THE ART

OF

PERSUASION

THE ART

OF

PERSUASION

WINNING
Without Intimidation

Bob Burg

From National Bestselling Author of
The Go Giver

Tremendous Life Books
118 West Allen Street
Mechanicsburg, PA 17055
www.tremendouslifebooks.com

and
Sound Wisdom
167 Walnut Bottom Road
Shippensburg, PA 17257
www.soundwisdom.com

Previously published as *Winning Without Intimidation* by Executive Books, 1998.

Gender usage: The author feels strongly regarding the use of gender equality in his writing. The pronouns *his* and *her, he* and *she,* and *him* and *her* have been used interchangeably.

Trade Paper ISBN: 978-0-7684-1300-7
Hard Cover ISBN: 978-1-64095-119-8
Ebook ISBN: 978-0-7684-8700-8

For Worldwide Distribution, Printed in the U.S.A.
HC: 1 2 3 4 5 / 23 22 21 20 19
TP: 18 19 20 / 26 25 24 23

Dedication

To Mom and Dad, as always: I love you more than life itself, and treasure the fact that G-d chose me to be your son.

Dad: this is really *your* book. You are my hero and my mentor, and you've taught me these principles. In fact, you taught me these principles in the very best way possible: you have lived them every day! The work I do is simply carrying on your message.

Acknowledgments

This is the most difficult section for every book I write, because no one is more aware than I of how little I actually know, and that producing a book is very much a team effort. As always, I'll do my best to mention some of the key players, realizing that there will be many people not mentioned who should be. To those inadvertently left out, please forgive me and know that you are in my heart.

My family: you are always there for me with love, support, and encouragement.

Kathy Zader: you are my de facto business partner and the person who makes my company run. You continue to amaze me with your ability to do...well, everything. And mainly, by how you always make me look good. You are truly the Agent 99 to my Maxwell Smart.

Ilene Vucovich: you are a true team player with exceptional organizational skills and, even more importantly, a sense of loyalty second to none.

All the full- and part-time team members at Burg Communications, Inc.: thank you. Teamwork is what makes our team work.

John David Mann: teaming up with you to write the Go-Giver books was one of the best ideas I ever had, if I do say so myself. Thanks for adding your light editorial-sandpapering touch to this book.

Special friends, mentors, and heroes who have taught me so much and made such a huge difference in my life: there are too many of you to even begin mentioning you one by one. You know who you are. I only hope you know how much I appreciate you.

My clients: without you I wouldn't have an audience and the pleasure of involvement in such a wonderful, rewarding, and fun career such as this.

The positive persuasion legends, such as Dale Carnegie, Les Giblin, Abraham Lincoln, and so many others: as far as I'm concerned, you are our national treasures.

And finally, you, dear reader: for your participation, feedback, and involvement. With me, this book is only an idea; you are what completes the process.

Contents

Introduction

What if you could get what you want…*when* you want it…and from *whom* you want it—including the difficult people you all too often come across?

Would that interest you?

Would that excite you?

Practically everyone would love to have that ability, wouldn't they?

In studying some of the most successful men and women in history—Benjamin Franklin, Harriet Beecher Stowe, Abraham Lincoln, Mother Teresa, Mohandas Gandhi— we notice they share many common characteristics. Each of these winners had a burning desire, coupled with great

THE ART OF PERSUASION

creativity, and a total, unshakable belief in their mission or cause. One trait which stands above all the rest is their ability to win people over to their way of thinking through *the art of positive persuasion.*

According to *Webster's Dictionary,* to win means *to succeed or prevail in a contest or effort; to triumph; to be victorious.* To persuade is *to cause someone to do something, especially by reasoning, urging, or inducement.* Persuasion means to *prevail upon.* When we persuade effectively, it results in others taking action. When we persuade positively, it results in others taking positive action. Persuasion does not mean manipulation.

In his book *The Art of Talking So That People Will Listen,* Dr. Paul W. Swets writes, "Manipulation aims at control, not cooperation. It results in a win/lose situation. It does not consider the good of the other party... In contrast to the manipulator, the persuader seeks to enhance the self-esteem of the other party. The result is that people respond better because they are treated as responsible, self-directing individuals."

Throughout the pages of this book, you will find skills, techniques, and attitudes of positive persuasion that, as you learn, internalize and apply them, will make your life a whole lot easier, a whole lot less stressful, and a whole lot more fun.

(By the way, although I've been using the phrase "positive persuasion," the truth is that, as Dr. Swets has pointed out, persuasion by its very nature is positive—so from here on in, I'll simply use the term *persuasion* with the assumption that we're talking about something that is both positive and benevolent.)

Am I actually telling you that winning through persuasion is simply a skill? That anyone can learn to be a winning communicator?

Yes, I am.

I know, that sounds like a bit of a stretch. It really isn't. Persuasion skills are not something most of us are born with. Like riding a bicycle, driving a car, or fly-fishing, it is a skill you can learn. And it is not only a skill you can learn, it is one you can master.

Mastering the art of persuasion. Now *that's* exciting!

I've heard it said that success in most areas of life is based 10 percent on technical skills and 90 percent on people skills. From my experience, those figures ring absolutely true. In *The Art of Persuasion*, you'll learn those people skills necessary to ensure that you have all the advantages needed to put that 90 percent to work for you and for others, too; day in, day out in all areas of your life and work.

I wish I could take credit for inventing these skills. I can't. I've been very fortunate not only to read and study the great masters of winning persuasion, but to grow up with and learn by example from many of them as well. I've simply taken what I've learned and applied and put it all into a simple, easy-to-use resource. Anyone can learn these skills and apply and benefit from them for the rest of their lives.

Here is one important key to knowing you are doing this right. If, in the process of persuading a person to your side of an issue, they feel as good about it as you do, then you have not bullied, coerced, or manipulated. You see, genuine winners are those people who can get what they want from others in such a way that's of genuine and lasting benefit *to everyone involved*—whether it's better seats at the theater or ball game, more cooperation at work and at home, the accomplishment of your life-long dream or a variety of other advantages. I call this *winning without intimidation*. Yes, you can indeed obtain satisfaction and be loved while you're doing it. That's power; that's influence.

There's absolutely no reason to live or work as a person who's constantly picked on, emotionally put down, taken advantage of, or made to settle for less in any way. And there's certainly no reason to ever resort to bullying or manipulating people to get what you really want, either.

What would your life be like if the benefits promised in the subtitle of this book really were attainable, and if you truly could master them? They are—and you can.

I'm sure you've heard the phrase, "win/win." Let's do that for greater results than anyone ever thought possible. Let's create a world where everybody wins through *the art of persuasion*.

Best of success,
Bob Burg

1

Winning Without Intimidation

From the very first moment, early in the morning, when we first hit the highways and side streets of the "real world" out there, right up to the moment we return home again at night, we are often faced with people who seem to be specially trained and highly motivated to irritate, aggravate and infuriate us with their unhelpful, downright rude and rotten attitudes.

Sometimes it's the person next to us on the train with his newspaper spread out over two-thirds of *our* space, or the waitperson at the coffee shop or lunch counter who can't *wait* for us to leave. The surly guy at the, ahem, *customer service* desk. The preoccupied prospect you're calling who can barely give you the time of day. Your boss...your employees...the hit-and-run hopeful who helps you spill your coffee on the way to work...the list goes on and on.

Please don't get me wrong. It's not that everyone alive is nasty or an example of bad manners. But I read recently that 61 *percent* of the American public thinks their fellow citizens are rude! If they're right, that means that if you're not already being mistreated by the guy or gal to your left, then as soon as you turn to the guy or gal to your right, you probably will be.

I'm not sure if I buy that statistic. In my experience, most people are genuinely nice and will treat us well, if given half the chance. If not downright benevolent, at least benign. But they're not the ones who make our pursuit of happiness difficult. There are "most people"...and then there are those people whose mission in life (at least at the moment you happen to encounter them) seems to be making *your* life difficult.

So what do you do?

There are only two choices. One choice is to get down on their level, and crouch right down there in the gutter of the most abrasive and nastiest of people "skills." You can fight with them, argue with them, one-up them. Show 'em who they're dealing with, show 'em they can't push you around. Of course, if you do that, you still might not get what you want. And even if you do, you'll probably end up feeling worse about yourself, and in the process make an enemy for life, making any encounters with that person in the future even more difficult, painful, and problematic.

And then there's the other choice: *You can win*.

When I use the word "win," I don't mean the kind of winning that works by making the other person lose. Far from it. In fact, just the opposite. By "win" I mean *getting what you want from that person while making him or her feel really good about you and the situation at hand.* And what a great feeling of accomplishment that is!

My Dad always taught us the words of the Talmudic sage Simeon ben Zoma: "Who is a mighty person?"

And the answer?

"One who can control his emotions and make of an enemy a friend."

That's just what we're going to learn how to do in this book. It will increase your effectiveness with loved ones, strangers, associates, and anyone else with whom you come in contact in all kinds of situations.

The skills and methods I'll show you don't work only for me. These ideas are totally transferable to anyone—and easily duplicated by anyone, too. I hear success stories all the time from people who've learned to apply these methods. Some have just recently acquired or learned them at one of my seminars, while others have already been practicing them for a long time.

And these methods *really work.* That's one reason I suggest reading and reviewing the book several times, until you begin to internalize the information so it becomes part of your being, a genuine part of who you are. You could simply read over and learn the information, and if you do, you will indeed see an improvement. But once it becomes a part of you—your heart, your essence—without your having to think about it, you'll see your interpersonal effectiveness go through the roof.

The key to over-the-top success in this endeavor is to internalize what you read throughout this book. Once you do this, I guarantee you'll be amazed by the results. You'll gain all the benefits promised in the title, plus many more, including such surprises as receiving more money from people and more satisfaction from situations than you previously thought possible.

There are several other books you'll notice I refer to and recommend. Purchase them, if you'd like, and then internalize their information as well. And the very best thing you can do to master this material is to share these methods with others. One of the most effective ways to learn and internalize information is to teach it.

One of my favorite books is *How To Have Confidence and Power in Dealing With People*, by Les Giblin. Giblin says that what counts is a way to get along with people, or deal with people, that will bring you personal satisfaction and at the same time not trample on the egos of those you deal with. I love his definition of *human relations*: the science of dealing with people in such a way that your ego and their ego both remain intact. Isn't that great?

Giblin also says that influencing people is an art, not a gimmick—and he's 100 percent correct. Oh, sure, every so often a gimmick, as insincere as it may be, is going to work. However, by relying on superficial gimmicks, you're lowering the odds of consistent success in the long run. Do you really want to internalize a gimmick and make it part of who you are?

What I'm writing about in this book are not gimmicks; they are the principles of *the art of persuasion*. You'll probably be surprised to find that part of what we look at here will be familiar, because you've heard or read it before, possibly many times. But we'll take it a step further. I'm going to show how these principles can be applied as part of a *system* to work consistently and effortlessly throughout your entire life and work.

Let's begin by looking at a couple of basic principles which will help you understand people, why they act the way they do and how that can lead to increasing your own effectiveness in this area.

How We Make Decisions

First, here's one of the most basic principles of human nature which, if you can keep in mind continually, will help you immeasurably in your quest toward mastering *The Art of Persuasion*.

If you are now, or ever have been, involved in any type of professional sales, you already know the following principle. It was one of the first principles you learned in Sales Training 101. This principle is universal: It holds true for me, for you, and for practically everyone else on this planet, even though we are often the first ones to deny it, even while we're in the act of doing it.

All right, enough suspense; here's the principle:

We human beings act out of emotion, not logic.

Again, if you've had any type of sales training you already know this and you've had all kinds of real-world examples thrown at you to prove it's true. You understand it, and you believe it. That's important, because from now on, I want you to always keep it in mind:

We human beings act out of emotion, not logic.

I believe we all are in sales, whether we do it professionally or not. After all, we sell ideas all the time, don't we? People sell their spouses on doing what *they* want them to do. Parents sell children on being respectful, going to bed on time, and staying away from drugs. Children sell parents on buying them that toy or letting them stay out past eleven o'clock. Teachers sell students on learning, and students sell teachers on excuses as to why they didn't hand in the assignment. Yes, clearly: we all sell.

Still, if you're not actually involved directly in selling a product or service, it may be hard to accept the idea that we all buy things based on our emotions, and not on our logic. After all, you consider yourself to be a very logical person, don't you? And you probably are. I'd like to think the same about myself.

However, no matter how logical we are, here is something you and I share in common: we both buy on *emotion*.

This is an extremely important concept. It is the basis for everything I'll be sharing with you in this book. The reason I'm stressing the point is that it would be very difficult for you to learn (let alone master) the methods in these pages without having first embraced this concept.

Here's how it works. We make decisions based on several types of emotions, but they all boil down to these two main drives:

a) The desire for pleasure.

b) The avoidance of pain.

We decide what we're going to do (buy or not buy a product, service, concept, idea) based on those two factors. Then we back up our emotional decision with a logical reason. It's known as rationalization.

Ultra-successful entrepreneur Dexter Yager says, "If we break up the word rationalize, it becomes *rational lies*." That's what we sometimes tell ourselves, isn't it?

Let me give you an excellent example of an emotional buying decision backed by the "logic" of *rational lies*:

Years ago, in my "salad days" (so called mainly because that was about all I could afford to eat), I faced a dilemma pretty much every day at about five o'clock in the afternoon: *I was starving*. The challenge was that I didn't have much money, so I always ate what cost the least. Not surprisingly, I never felt quite satisfied after the meal.

One day, on my way home from work, I passed a steakhouse. *Mm-mm*. The very thought of that succulent, juicy steak, that baked potato loaded with butter and sour cream, the soft, warm, freshly baked bread.... This was years ago, before we all became as concerned as we are today with fatty food intake. But you know what? I was so hungry, it wouldn't have mattered anyway!

I stopped in front of that steakhouse—but not to actually go in and eat. I knew I couldn't afford to do that, and that if I did, I would have hardly any money left until the next payday, and that was way far away. But...I could at least look at the place from the outside, couldn't I? I could just stand there and smell it at no charge...right?

Rational lie number one.

Then I thought, hey, why not go in and just look at a menu? You know, just see what they've got. After all, one day I'll actually be able to afford this kind of food, and gosh darn it, I need to be able to picture what it is I'm going to be eating, right? And that will give me more incentive to work even harder...right?

Rational lie number two.

Once inside the place, I thought—and this was *kind of* true—you know what? If I were to eat a hearty meal like this, it would give me the strength to work even harder the next day, wouldn't it? All that protein in the meat would be good for me. After all, I didn't want to get too thin. And the potato: why, the skin alone had vitamins that everyone needs....

Rational lie number three.

Those thoughts were all rational, weren't they? Sure they were. And they were all lies. They added up to the logic I used to back up my *emotional decision*—which was to sit down and tear into that steak. (By the way, it was the best tasting steak I ever ate.)

Have you ever done something like that? Sure you have. We all do it, all the time. Not necessarily to that extent. (At least I hope not!) But think about every major decision or choice you've ever made: buying your home or car...getting married...leaving a secure job...using your savings or mortgaging your home to start your own business where the risk was greater and the hours longer.

Was any of that based on logic—*really*—or was it pure emotion?

Over the next few days, observe every decision of substance that you make. I suspect you'll find that they are all, every one of them, based on emotion. What's more, every one of them will have something to do with either your desire for pleasure, or your avoidance of pain, or both. It's what we do: we will back up our emotional decisions by retrofitting them with our "make-sense" logic.

The Role Our Egos Play

Let's look a little more closely at those two major emotions, because this subject has everything to do with the art of persuasion. They are what make people tick.

What kinds of pleasure do we human beings pursue? Well, we all know about physical pleasures, such as sexual pleasure or the pleasure of eating something mouthwatering, like your favorite flavor of ice cream. And we certainly know about emotional pleasures, too, such as enjoying time with family and friends, or the fun of buying an exciting new toy. The list of possible pleasures we might anticipate and experience is endless. But for the moment, let's focus on one in particular: the pleasure of power when dealing with other people, which is part of the ego.

That is, the ego *they* have. (Oh, no, not us...*them.*)

Have you ever had an experience with negative, difficult people? Perhaps the person at the Registry of Motor Vehicles, the teller at the bank, the prospect who's listening to your sales presentation, the uncivil servant, your boss, a fellow employee, the police officer, anybody and everybody else. Here is what they all have in common: if they're flexing their power *over you*, it's because in some way it brings pleasure to their ego.

What about the avoidance of pain? And I'm not talking only about physical pain. In fact, physical pain is the least important to consider, for the sake of this book, since we're not looking to beat anyone up in order to get what we want. (I want you to win through *persuasion*, not *intimidation*.)

What kind of pain would a person want to avoid? How about the pain associated with getting fired? The feeling of pain that accompanies change, or of taking the risk of initiative, especially when that's not normally a requirement of that person's job? What about the pain that comes with embarrassment? Or of looking bad, the pain of losing face?

In all of these situations and countless more like them, the ego comes into play. Ego is so important to all of us. You don't want to look bad to others, or to feel bad about yourself, do you? No one does. People respond or react to us emotionally for two reasons: either to gain a certain type of pleasure, or to avoid a certain type of pain.

And most of that response or reaction centers on the ego.

Speaking of those two words, *respond* and *react*, there is actually a vast difference between the two, and in a few moments we'll look at what that difference is and how you can use it to effectively and easily persuade for everyone's benefit.

Remember the story I told on myself earlier regarding that steak dinner? I was working on both emotions, wasn't I? The quest for pleasure—in reality, almost *desperately* wanting that meal; and the avoidance of pain—being *sooo* hungry my stomach actually ached. No wonder I ended up succumbing and shelling out for that pricey dinner that I couldn't afford. I told myself that, *anyone* else would've done the exact same thing. And it was all *rational lies*!

And here's a thought: What if I had made the decision to go to that expensive restaurant (which I clearly could not afford) in order to bring a date there with the plan of impressing her? Would that have involved my ego as well? You bet it would.

Roles We Play in Relationships

Let's set another foundation regarding a basic human principle, *cause of action*.

I first learned about this through the book, *I'm Okay, You're Okay*, by Dr. Thomas Harris. Dr. Harris points out that each of us takes on one of three personality traits or characteristics during every conversation or interaction. By now, many have been introduced to this concept, but I'd like to describe what he wrote and what it means to me in my own words here. (For a deeper understanding of this topic, I suggest buying his book *Transactional Analysis*. Another excellent book on this subject is *Games People Play* by Dr. Eric Berne, widely considered the father of transactional analysis.)

Each of us is capable of displaying three distinct personality states: the *Parent*, the *Adult*, and the *Child*. These are states taken on, so to speak, depending upon what we are feeling at any specific moment. The following is my interpretation of these three states and how they relate to the art of positive persuasion.

The Child in all of us is perceived as the victim. As the Child we feel like a baby, put down, blamed, punished, controlled. As a result, we are angry and looking to get even. The Child wants to get even with the person who assumes the role of the Parent.

The Parent in all of us is usually a victim of his or her own upbringing, biases, and environment. People in the

Parent role mean well, they just don't recognize their own negative communication. They don't realize they're putting somebody else down. They don't realize they're making the other person feel bad.

The Adult in all of us (which is the ideal) is the positive negotiator, the communicator, the respectful, honest, active listener, the one in the situation who is trustworthy, who is easy to love and respect.

Within any relationship or transaction between two people, there are typically combinations of all three of these states. Somebody else criticizes, condemns, or talks down to you; they are the Parent and you are the Child. In that situation, you have to know that it's not something to be taken personally (as difficult as that may be)—but first you have to bring yourself up to the Adult level in order to even begin to put yourself in the position for a win/win.

At the same time, you have to watch yourself and make sure you don't come across like the Parent, talking down to that other person and putting them in the position of the Child. They may react negatively toward you because of the fear of (i.e., avoidance of) pain, be that hurt, embarrassment, loss of face, or some other variation of pain.

Ideally, you want every transaction with another person to be on the level of Adult to Adult. Easy? No. Possible? Absolutely—with awareness, practice, and work.

It's very important to keep in mind the human factor: you can't expect others to act as you do just because you know what you're doing and are in the state of mind to do it. Don't feel put down if the other person doesn't respond "correctly." Through the material we cover in this book, you'll learn how to get them there. It takes time and effort, but you can do it. Please don't get frustrated. Okay, you can get frustrated—but keep at it anyway! The rich results are worth it.

The best way to overcome frustration is to make a game out of it. As you become more proficient at mastering the art of persuasion in order to get what you want, when you want it, and from whom you want it, you'll be absolutely amazed at the fun you'll have with it.

I'm excited for you already!

Responding Versus Reacting

One idea we should touch upon now is that difference we spoke of earlier between *responding* and *reacting*. I first learned about this from Zig Ziglar, the internationally acclaimed author and speaker. This wisdom of Zig's really hit home for me. It alone has probably kept me out of more trouble than I care to remember.

So, according to Zig: *to respond is positive; to react is negative.*

Allow me to paraphrase an example Zig used that beautifully makes this point: When going to the doctor after taking some medication that worked, the doctor might say, "Ah, you *responded* well to the medication." On the other hand, if you go in breathing heavily, with your face broken out in bumps and hives, the doctor will probably say something like, "It seems the medication has caused a bad *reaction.*"

You *responded* well...you had a *reaction*. Vivid difference, isn't it?

It's the same in any relationship, transaction with another human being or situation in life. If you *respond to* it, you've thought it out and acted in a mature, positive fashion. If you *react to* it, you've let it be in control and get the best of you.

Throughout this book, I'll focus on *responding to* situations and challenges with people so that you can stay in control of yourself and the situation. That way, you'll be in a position to help both yourself and the other person to a mutually beneficial conclusion.

Tact: The Language of Strength

Here I need to mention one more key concept that will be at the very heart of everything we explore in this book: *tact*.

My Dad defines tact as "the language of strength." (In the book *It's Not About You*, which I coauthored with John David Mann, there is an entire chapter called "The Language of Strength," and it has my Dad's wisdom on the subject of tact laced throughout its pages.)

Tact is simply the ability to say something or make a point in such a way that the other person is not offended, and indeed, actually embraces your suggestion. Now *that's* strength. Another word for tact is *diplomacy*. Real-life diplomats are responsible for employing tact in such a way as to keep their countries from going to war with each other. We may not have that responsibility, but we all have ample opportunities to serve as diplomats in our own lives, too.

If we could listen to a recording of what we say in everyday conversations, we might be amazed at our lack of tact and sensitivity in the way we relate to others. There's a good deal of truth in the saying, "You can catch more flies with honey than you can with vinegar."

Let's make an agreement, you and I, that we'll analyze the way we talk to others for just twenty-one days. And after that, twenty-one more. At that point, it will have become a habit, especially after you realize the dramatically positive effect it has in and on your life. If you feel you don't know how to do that—no problem. This book will supply you with the correct wording, attitude, and phraseology.

A quick review:

- Human beings take action out of emotion (the desire for pleasure, the avoidance of pain) and back up that emotion with logic. We rationalize, telling ourselves *rational lies*.

- Ego is each person's individual sense of self. We must honor that throughout the process of *winning without intimidation*.

- People take on one of three emotional states during every conversation or interaction: the Parent, the Adult, or the Child.

- We have a choice to *respond* or to *react*. Responding is positive and will add to your success. Reacting is negative and will have the opposite effect.

- A major player in *the art of persuasion* is tact!

2

Learning the Art
of Persuasion

Throughout this book, we'll be looking at both long-range and short-range ideas for turning you into a master persuader.

If you can establish certain feelings about you in other people, what I refer to as "know you, like you and trust you" feelings, that will cause your future battles or challenges to be already half-won. This is a very important aspect of this book, since there are a certain cast of characters in your life, both major and minor players, that you must be able to deal with in a positive way again and again.

We'll work on that.

Then there are those short-range, one-time shots you encounter where you need to take on a challenging situation with a person you may never see again, but from whom you need something, and need it *now*. We'll work on that one as well, and to me, that's a lot of fun. Let's begin with some of those long-range ideas.

Thoughtfulness

It's a simple idea. No really incredible skills needed here, so let's just consider it a good warm-up exercise. If you employ the idea of thoughtfulness regularly and religiously, every day and in every circumstance possible, it will give you a head start toward accomplishing all that you are reading about in this book.

I read an interesting story in the book *The Best of Bits & Pieces*, compiled by Arthur Lenehan, that highlighted several acts of thoughtfulness. The main point being illustrated was that "thoughtfulness is a habit—a way of life well worth cultivating and practicing."

Thoughtfulness doesn't necessarily come naturally. Thoughtfulness needs to be worked on, cultivated and practiced enough so that you internalize these *thoughtful thoughts* into your very being. And that makes sense, because, let's face it, it's often easier *not* to be thoughtful. As the late master teacher Jim Rohn used to say, "Easy to do … easy not to do." It's up to you to initiate and cultivate this habit in the short term that will pay huge dividends in the long term.

Yes: *huge* dividends in terms of becoming the persuader you desire to be. And between you and me, it's a better, more fulfilling way to live life, as well.

One part of that *Bits & Pieces* story pointed out that thoughtful people don't wait for opportunities to be thoughtful, they imaginatively create numerous opportunities to make life brighter, smoother, and more enjoyable for those around them.

How do we do this?

One thing that works for me is take time to hold a door open for someone—male or female, it doesn't matter. They'll appreciate you for it. It doesn't take long, but it makes a big difference, both for that person and for us as we make it into a habit that gradually makes us into a more thoughtful person.

When a baby near you in a restaurant is making just a bit more noise than is comfortable, and you see the parent looking a little embarrassed, smile and comment on how cute the baby is. You might be thinking, "Baloney! That parent should get that kid out of there!" Maybe they should—but are you looking to be right, or *make the sale*— the "sale" in this case being the strengthening of a new and very productive habit.

Another part of the story said, "The thoughtful person is quick to pay a well-deserved compliment, or to send a prompt note of congratulations to someone who has received a promotion, an honor, or some special recognition."

Thoughtful people park a bit farther from the entrance of the store or post office, leaving the nearer space for someone who doesn't get around as easily as they do. You might ask, "Why should I do that? Nobody will know why I'm parking a bit farther away, so I won't receive any benefit."

Let me offer two reasons. First, it's simply the right thing to do, and it will make you feel better about yourself and will show up in your attitude toward others. And number two, *thoughtfulness is a habit*, and as such, it can be cultivated and mastered. Your choice of parking spots is one more way to so cultivate and master.

Another thoughtful act is to give proper credit for an idea—and in that spirit, let me point out that the contributing author of that particular story in *The Best of Bits & Pieces* was William A. Ward.

Mr. Ward, the contribution you made was to help me realize that thoughtfulness is just a habit—one that can serve everyone in mastering the art of persuasion, and one for which I thank you!

Feeling the Other Person's Feelings

Let's do another warm-up exercise. This will help you in your newfound ability to *respond to* situations and people, instead of simply *reacting*.

Remember the Native American adage about walking a mile in another person's moccasins? What does that really mean, and how can you use that wonderful piece of advice to further your mastery of persuasion?

What if a person says or does something that offends you or doesn't fit into your model of how you like things to be done? Instead of reacting, what if you responded by immediately asking yourself, "What could possibly be happening in that person's life that has given her a major case of halitosis of the personality?" (Or, as Zig Ziglar would say, a "hardening of the attitudes.")

Imagine a day in the life of this unhappy person, and maybe you can get a better idea of what she needs from you right now in order to make her feel good about herself and want to help you. Only then can the persuasion process begin.

Maybe that person came from a negative environment. Perhaps there was no communication in her childhood home, or perhaps she was even mistreated. At school, perhaps she was rejected by her peers. And mind you, I'm not trying make excuses for her or give her an "out" for her not to accept responsibility for her actions. I'm simply trying to explore what might be the facts of her story. As an underachiever with a hard background and a terrible self-image, perhaps she then had it no better in her adult life. Today, she hates her job, and doesn't feel much better about her husband. And her kid just got thrown into a juvenile detention center for shoplifting.

How do you feel about her now? Can you understand her lousy attitude just a little better?

The situation with this person might not be that bad ... or it might be worse. If you can simply consider another possibility, you can *respond* to that person and her actions with compassion and understanding instead of *reacting* with hate and anger.

Here's a very powerful story along these same lines:

In his perennial best-seller, *The 7 Habits of Highly Effective People*, Stephen R. Covey shares an experience he had one Sunday morning on a New York subway. Sundays are about the only time subways are peaceful in New York, and this morning was no exception: people were sitting quietly, some reading their papers, some lost in thought, others cat-napping as the train pulled into the station.

Suddenly the scene was shattered as two boisterous children burst into the car. Loud and obnoxious, they were yelling back and forth, racing around, even grabbing other people's newspapers. They were totally out of control—yet the man who came in with them, presumably their father, just sat there, staring at the floor of the subway car, oblivi-ous. Talk about thoughtless! Everybody in that car was ir-ritated by the children's behavior and the father's lack of responsibility.

Can you get a sense of what it must have felt like being one of the people on that subway? What would your reac-tion have been?

Well, Dr. Covey—whose patience had finally ended—turned to the man and said (with what I imagine was considerable restraint), "Sir, your children are really disturbing a lot of people. I wonder if you could control them a little more?"

The man looked up and around for the first time and softly said to Covey, "Oh, you're right. I guess I should do something about it." Then he explained that they had just come from the hospital where, only an hour ago, the chil-dren's mother had died. He said he didn't know what to think—and he guessed they didn't either.

Wham! In an instant, Dr. Covey's *reaction* changed to a totally different *response.*

"Your wife just died. Oh, I'm so sorry!" he said, now with sympathy and compassion. "Can you tell me about it? What can I do to help?"

With practice, we won't even need to be shocked by the person's true story for us to change our attitude toward them. If, with practice, we continually make an effort to put ourselves in the other's person's moccasins, we can actually *consciously reframe* the situation. We'll then approach that person in a completely different, more positive, and more productive way.

And we'll have taken a giant step in the persuasion process.

People Do Things for Their Reasons, Not for Ours

In his awesome book, *How to Win Friends and Influence People* (really a *must* read/study), Dale Carnegie talks about the fact that people do things for their reasons—not for ours. If they're going to do something, it's because there's a benefit to their doing it.

Oh, I know: people wake up early every morning to go to work even though they don't want to. But they get up every morning to go to work because they want the benefit of something more than the great feeling of staying in bed— namely a paycheck at the end of the week.

What about people who do charity work for others? They're not deriving a benefit from it, are they? Sure they are! The benefit they receive is the good feeling that comes with doing good and with taking action that aligns with their beliefs and principles.

Mr. Carnegie was right: people do things for their own reasons—even if that reason is simply to feel better about themselves. Better than the feeling they would have had if they didn't do that good deed.

If there's something we need somebody to do for us that they don't *have* to do, then we had better be ready to give them a personal benefit, so that they feel better about doing that particular thing for us than they would feel by not doing it.

People Will Do What They Think You Expect Them to Do

People will typically behave the way they think you expect them to behave, and they will act the way they think you expect them to act. That can work for you either positively or negatively, depending upon your expectations.

Here's a great example you may have heard before. Not only is this a true story, but I suspect it's actually been reenacted thousands of times over the years to prove and reprove the point.

A grade school teacher was going to be away for a few days. Before leaving, she met with the substitute to fill her in about the children and what she should expect of them. She told the substitute that Johnny was the smartest; Joanne, the most helpful; Jimmy and Susie, the class troublemakers (watch out for them!); David never paid attention (better keep him on his toes!); and so on.

A few days later, when she returned and asked how everything had gone in her absence, the substitute told her that everything she had said turned out to be exactly true. Johnny *was* the smartest, and Joanne the most helpful.

Jimmy and Susan were no end of trouble, and David did have a difficult time paying attention.

What was remarkable about this report was that *the teacher had made the whole thing up.* She chose kids at random and gave them completely made-up personalities. It didn't matter. Not only had the substitute transferred her expectations into the minds and hearts of the children, but she acted toward them in such a way as to elicit from each of them exactly the behaviors she expected them to exhibit.

It reminds me of the old story of the Quaker villages. In every village, there was an old gentleman placed at the gate whose job it was to greet strangers as they entered the village. He would welcome them warmly and answer all their questions. When the visitors asked (as they invariably did), "What are the people like here?" the old man always asked them in return, "Why, what were they like where you came from?"

If the stranger replied the people where he came from kept to themselves, were suspicious and rather cold by nature, the old man would nod and reply, "They are the same here."

If the stranger said the people where he came from were friendly, open and warm-hearted, the old man would nod and reply, "They are the same here."

In his excellent book, *How to Have Confidence and Power in Dealing with People,* another highly-recommended read, Les Giblin cites many examples of how this works just as predictably in the real world of here and now, and he quotes the great British statesman Sir Winston Churchill: "I have found that the best way to get another to acquire a virtue is to *impute it* to him."

Both for long-term and immediate results, when you want to bring out a response in a person that meets your needs, act toward that person as though that is exactly how you expect them to respond. And when you approach a person for something you need, approach them *believing they're going to want to give it to you*.

Please understand, I'm not saying that simply because you think about it, that's what will automatically happen. Not at all. But here is what *will* happen: When you pre-determine someone's actions in your own mind, *you* then take on the corresponding attitude. In other words, if you expect them to be kind and helpful, you project gratitude. And when that person is approached by one who expresses gratitude toward them, what do you suppose the chances are that they will act with kindness and helpfulness? Exactly. If you doubt this, then please suspend your doubt and do this with sincerity several times. I guarantee you'll walk away in amazement!

This is another basic principle that I'll refer to throughout this book, so please keep it in mind: to a surprising degree, people act toward you the way you *expect* them to. It happens to be one of the most powerful principles and methods of all, and we need to practice applying it until it becomes habit.

Politeness, Patience, and Persistence

It was late morning on the day of a big exposition. I would be speaking the following day, and I, along with several other people, had rented booth space where we would market my series of audio and video tapes and books.

Ah, the books...and there was the challenge: *they weren't there!*

I had just found out about the situation as I checked in at my hotel and picked up a message that the woman who was running our booth had left for me at the front desk. This was in Toronto, Ontario, and since my books were sent via ground transportation from my publisher's Ontario division, there should not have been any challenge at all. But there was—and it needed to be handled right away, or else the trip would be an expensive disaster!

I called the Metro Toronto Convention Center and spoke to the switchboard operator, who, as it turned out, had no idea how to connect me to the area where the booths were located. Not only did she not know the answer: she apparently wasn't interested in going out of her way to find it for me, either.

What does one do in a situation like this?

Take a breath—and be *polite, patient,* and *persistent.*

Why *polite?* Because it will disarm the person, and it is not only a proper way to act, but also an effective and profitable one, too.

Dick Biggs, in his book *If Life Is a Balancing Act, Why Am I So Darn Clumsy?*, quotes B. C. Forbes as saying, "Politeness is the hallmark of the gentleman and the gentlewoman. No single, positive characteristic will help you to advance—whether in business or society—as politeness."

Why *patient?* Because we all realize that many, ahem, "service" people have gotten into the habit when dealing with the public (many of whom, let's face it, can be rather impolite, impatient and rude themselves) of doing as little as possible and then hanging up the phone. Patience comes in handy when things don't work themselves out immediately after your first request.

And then? Then let your *persistence* take over.

So here's the sequence:

Be polite to that person and even thank them. "Oh, thank you. I appreciate your effort in looking into it for me. How would we be able to find out where they are and what their extension is?" With a smile in your voice, you might add, "I'm in really big trouble if I can't locate the right person."

This time the operator answers, no more helpfully but with more concern than coldness in her voice, "I don't know."

Be patient. This is just how she's used to doing things.

Now you say, "I really appreciate your help. I know you're doing your best. Is it possible for you to look through your listing of extensions and take a couple shots at it? I don't want to bother you, I just have to find that booth."

At this point, she is going to make an emotional decision based on the avoidance of pain: the pain of having to keep talking to this polite, patient, and persistent person who obviously is *not* going to stop until he receives the information he needs.

You're probably wondering what happened in Toronto.

Yes, the switchboard operator finally tracked down the extension, and I was able to get the woman at the booth to find out from the loading dock exactly what happened. A few phone calls and several hours later, my books arrived, and the day was saved.

Remember the three P's—especially with people who are not usually required to go out of their way to help. You must be Polite, Patient, *and* Persistent.

Motivating the Unmotivated

Four days later, after that Toronto convention was over, I was faced with another dilemma. Due to a logistical challenge, I had to personally move all the books that had not sold down to the loading dock so we could have them shipped from there. Getting the books down there wasn't that big of a challenge—but once the books and I were there, it was clear that the fellow at the dock saw himself in the role of the working man who wasn't about to be pushed around by some guy in a suit.

I should have worn jeans.

When I first saw him, I couldn't tell whether he was one of the drivers or the guy running the operation. He was sitting on a chair reading a newspaper and drinking coffee, not looking like he was working too hard. That should have tipped me off. Yup, he was the boss!

Here's an important tip to keep in mind: If you don't know, always give the person you approach a more prestigious title than he or she may actually have. Even if they correct you, they'll love you for it—and it will begin the persuasion process on a very positive note.

If you think the person with whom you're speaking is the secretary, ask if she's the office manager. Not only will she appreciate your over-crediting her, but if it turns out she *is* the office manager and you ask if she's the secretary, you've started out with one big strike against you.

If you think the person is a host, ask if he's the manager. If you think she's the salesperson, ask if she's the sales manager.

So here I was, facing this gentleman of indeterminate position, whose help I needed. What I *should* have asked was, "Excuse me, are you the operations director?" But did I? Nope. Before giving myself a chance to think it through, I heard the following words fly from my lips: "Hi, are you one of the drivers?"

Oops. Now, I don't know why I did that. It must have been a case of temporary insanity, because I *never* do that. But I did. And naturally, he was not happy—at all.

"I'm the supervisor," he replied indignantly.

From there, however, I was able to "save the sale," the sale in this case being for him to agree to make the call to the correct shipping company, help me label the boxes correctly, and then agree to be responsible for the boxes until they were picked up. The condensed version of this transaction is:

I apologized immediately and said, "Of course, I should have known you are the supervisor!" Then I extended my hand and said, "I'm Bob Burg," and asked him his name. He told me, and I then referred to him as Mister So-and-So for the remainder of our conversation. Most people aren't used to being addressed that politely and respond very positively to being shown such respect. At the first opportunity, when he addressed me as "Mister Burg," I said, "Please, call me Bob," which he then did—but I continued to call him Mister So-and-So. (No, I did *not* actually call him, "Mister So-and-So," I used his real last name!)

Treating that supervisor the way I did put him in a position of power and respect—something that I am guessing he rarely encounters from a *suit*.

I then gave him even more of a power position by saying, "I understand that helping me isn't your job, and I wouldn't blame you if you can't do it, but I could really use your help."

He grudgingly asked what I needed, and I took it one step at a time. Every few minutes, when it felt appropriate, I asked him questions about himself: how he got started in the business, was he from this area, his family, and so forth, just some non-invasive, get-to-know-you-a-little questions. (It's important that doing this doesn't come off like you're giving a person the third degree: there is a fine line between being friendly and being nosey.)

Mister So-and-So began warming up to me.

"I really appreciate your help," I commented. "I have to tell ya, a lot of people nowadays just wouldn't take the time to put themselves out like this." He smiled with what seemed a newfound pride in himself and his job. He warmed up some more.

Before long he was taping my boxes, stacking them, and personally speaking with the operator at the shipping company on my behalf. He ended up doing a lot of work, all of which I greatly appreciated. He really helped me out, and he felt good about it, too—and I made a new friend. I also gave him a tip, which he rightly earned. At first he refused to take it, but I insisted. He thanked me for buying his lunch.

I won—and he won. *That* is the art of persuasion.

How would that scene have played out if instead, I had tried to throw my weight around? What if, say, I had threatened to talk to his boss if I didn't get the help I needed?

It's hard to say for sure. Maybe he'd have done the work I needed, maybe not. If he did, it most likely would have taken longer and not have been done as well. Who knows whether those boxes would have ever actually made it safely back to the publisher.

I'll tell you one thing we *do* know for sure: whatever he would have done or not done, it wouldn't have felt a *win* to him—and I wouldn't have gained a friend.

As it is, if I ever go back to that hotel again, I know he'll remember me, and I'll already be one big step ahead in the game.

"Thank You" in Advance Is the Best Insurance Policy You Can Buy

It's great to thank people after they do something nice for you. It's even more powerful to thank them *before* they do something for you.

"I really appreciate you taking the time to…" This is great insurance that they'll *make* the time to do whatever you want done. This may or may not be apocryphal, but I've heard that the practice of giving a "tip" to a restaurant waitperson was originally paid *before* the meal was served, and that the word tip itself was an acronym for To Insure Promptness. Historically factual or not, it's a great example of the principle, and it's a great way of describing it: as a kind of *insurance*. (Or extortion, depending upon how you look at it. I prefer insurance.)

As an example of a proper time to thank someone be-fore they start on the assignment, task or whatever, let's say you're talking to your prospect on the telephone. "Mr. Smith, thank you for taking a moment out of your schedule to speak with me."

Or, let's say you've just gotten the hotel manager on the phone, and you are about to inform her about a particular challenge you're having with your room: "Ms. Jackson, I appreciate your helping me with this unfortu-nate situation."

Maybe it's the mechanic who's about to work on your car: "Mr. Davis, thank you in advance for fixing this thing. Wow, do I depend on you to keep this car working right!"

Note that Mr. Davis hasn't yet worked on your car, Ms. Jackson doesn't even know what the challenge is yet, and Mr. Smith has not yet agreed to take time out of his busy schedule to speak with you. You're thanking them all ahead of time, *before* the fact.

This bring me to a crucial point: Your *thank you* must be said with sincerity and humility, and *not* as an implied de-mand, as it is sometimes taught. The same words delivered with a sense of entitlement ("I fully expect that you'll do this for me, because after all, it's your job, and you owe me") will come off as manipulative or overbearing.

Just take a moment to reflect on what you're most grate-ful for about this person, and go with that.

I once called a popular columnist at our local newspaper to ask her to lend her name to a charity event I was work-ing on. After I said hello and told her it was nice to speak with her, she began her part of the conversation by saying, "Thank you—I know you're going to be brief."

Not exactly the type of "Thank you" in advance I'm talking about here.

In fact, I immediately felt like being *really* brief—and hanging up right then and there. But a charity is a charity, and the cause I was representing was more important than my personal feelings (otherwise known as *ego*). I explained what I needed from her, and she turned me down.

What if, instead, she had said, "Mr. Burg, I'm always happy to talk to someone about supporting a worthy cause. Unfortunately, I'm in a bit of a rush right now and can't talk too long. How can I be of help?"

I would have gotten right to it, made my point quickly, and let her get right off the phone. She probably would not have volunteered her assistance in either case. But that way, I would have felt good about her and myself. As it was, the way she spoke to me did *not* make me feel good about myself—or about her.

And if by any chance you're thinking, "What does she care if you like her or not? She'll never need you for anything anyway."

Ahh, I'll answer that one later on in the chapter entitled, "The 7 Words that Can Come Back to Haunt You."

Acknowledging a Job Well Done Inspires a Lifetime of Repeated Efforts

Muriel is a sweet, elderly woman who works at the local supermarket in the deli section, where they make sandwiches for customers at lunchtime.

One day, I asked Muriel for a roast beef sandwich, adding, "extra lean, please." She did a really nice job, and after eating, I walked back over to the counter and genuinely thanked her—loud enough for all the other patrons and her coworkers to hear—for the "extra special nice job you did with my sandwich." Her eyes brightened and a smile came to her face.

From that day on, Muriel has always seemed to put a little extra meat on my sandwiches—and always very lean.

The point is this: acknowledge someone's effort after they do something for you once, and they'll typically take great pains to do it extra, *extra* special for you from then on.

The reason for this is very simple. First of all, most people just don't think enough to recognize a job well done, so your compliment is almost certain to be rare and very appreciated. Secondly, every time Muriel goes out of her way to make a great sandwich, she's making an emotional decision to achieve pleasure—the pleasure of being respected and appreciated, which is probably not an ordinary occurrence in her life. I can almost guarantee that's true, because Muriel is human, and sadly, appreciation and respect simply aren't ordinary occurrences in most people's lives.

On a plane back home from a speaking engagement, I asked the flight attendant if she could possibly substitute some of the items in my meal for some healthier foods. She obliged and put together a nice meal for me. I gave her so much genuine appreciation for her efforts that for the remainder of the flight, she kept wanting to know what more she could do for me.

What a nice cycle of success! Make a person feel good for their efforts, and they'll want to keep proving you right. It's been said, "Behavior that gets rewarded gets repeated." Remember, the appreciation you express must be genuine, or that person will only feel manipulated instead of appreciated.

There are few things in life more rewarding than genuinely making another person feel good about themselves. And the fact that this also results in your obtaining the results *you* desire makes it even *more* rewarding!

Handling Rude People on the Telephone

From sales prospects to government bureaucrats, with a zillion others in between, there are times when you make a necessary important call and are met by a person who is rude and apparently lives his life for the sole purpose of making *your* life miserable—especially during this particular call.

Let's say you've never met this person. You don't know him, and he doesn't know you. Either he's just not a very nice person, or he's having a particularly bad day. It's the same to you either way, isn't it? After all, what do you even know about him? This is a phone call between two strangers, and possibly the only one you'll ever have.

Let's look at how to handle that person and apply the art of persuasion.

Begin by making the conscious decision to *respond* to the situation, not to *react*. Most people in this situation would react: they'd argue with the person, insult him right back, try to match him word for word, and attitude for attitude, as if they were trying to beat him at his own game.

While that may provide a temporary pleasure, it won't work to your advantage in the long run. Not only will you probably *not* get what you need or want from that person, but you'll have made an enemy that might somehow come back to haunt you one day. And, let's face it: you'll have let yourself down knowing that you fell to his level. We've all been there.

Make the conscious decision to respond and not react.

Next, while he is talking, complaining, yelling, being generally unhelpful, or whatever, hear him out *without* interrupting. Then, and only then, you can very sincerely say, "I'm sorry, I must have said or done something to upset you. Did I?" And then be silent.

It may take a few seconds, but usually the other person will come right back with, "No, I'm sorry, I'm just having a bad day."

You can then respond with, "Boy, I've had some of those myself, it's always a lousy feeling." Then they're *yours*. They know you understand—and most people simply want to be heard and understood.

The same idea goes for handling an incoming upset call, with a slight twist. Let's say you represent a product or service and a customer calls to vehemently complain. This also works in person just as well, but let's pretend for right now that you're on the phone with them.

She calls and starts right in with everything that's wrong with you, your company, your product, your service. And, if there is anything else she can possibly find to complain about, she probably complains about that as well.

What do you do?

Choose to respond, not react.

You know what you do: you listen silently, first hearing her out completely. If it's an in-person situation, nod your head understandingly every so often. When she gets through, again let her know you *understand*.

"I understand you feel very strongly about this, and, quite frankly, I feel bad that this happened to you."

If appropriate, apologize. If not, don't. Just put yourself in that person's shoes. How would you feel if you were in her situation?

When you sincerely speak this way, you'll disarm her, because she has readied herself for the reaction she expects from the *average* person, who's going to shout right back at her out of defensiveness. Your calm, understanding response will come as a shock—and an unexpectedly pleasant one. Nine times out of ten, the person will calm down right then and you'll be able to have a conversation based on the Adult-to-Adult state of mind. If she doesn't calm down, go back to what you learned earlier about the three P's: be Polite, Patient, and Persistent. As long as you keep *yourself* in the Adult state, you'll outlast the other person's Parent or Child state and end up with a positive outcome.

One important point this example illustrates is the power of letting the other person have their say and hearing them out completely—*without* interrupting. This is another habit we all need to develop for any situation.

For me, this was always a tough one, but I've made dramatic improvements in this area since I began making a consistent, conscious effort to practice this. You see, no matter what I'm discussing, I naturally get so passionate about it that I just can't wait to get my point across, even if that means cutting someone off in mid-sentence. But doing so is worse than ineffective.

Whether you're discussing politics with a friend, taking part in a social group debate, or making a sales presentation to a prospect, you've got to let whoever is talking finish their point. If not, they'll become frustrated and angry, and no matter what point you make from that point on, they won't buy it.

Interrupting and ramming home your agenda is really a form of intimidation, even if it's not intended that way. Not only is it very difficult to persuade anyone while interrupting, it also makes it extremely likely that you'll never get a second chance to make your point with that person.

Don't interrupt. Just don't.

3

Know You,
Like You, Trust You

In my book *Endless Referrals*, I talk about what I call "the golden rule of networking." It's so central to this whole way of thinking and interacting with people that in our book *The Go-Giver*, John David Mann and I wrote about it again—and in our follow-up book, *Go-Givers Sell More*, we mentioned it yet again. It goes like this:

All things being equal, people will do business with, and refer business to, those people they know, like, and trust.

Modern technology has by and large leveled the playing fields of price and quality. Other factors aside, it's *the salesperson involved in the transaction* that determines whom the consumer will buy from and refer business to.

In the persuasion process, the "know you, like you, trust you" rule holds equally true. The difference here is that, if you're in a situation where you have never met the person from whom you need something, you have mere seconds to bring forth these feelings. If you can elicit those particular feelings toward yourself from the other person right off the bat, then you'll be more than halfway home.

If that person does not feel good about you, if they don't feel as though they know you, like you, and trust you, almost anything that *can* stand in the way, *will* stand in the way of your obtaining from this person what you desire.

The principles and methods we're discussing in this book are specifically designed to establish these positive and productive feelings in the other person quickly and effectively.

Ask for Advice

Depending upon the situation, asking a person for help or advice often endears you to him and he will be only too glad to help. To understand this, let's realize that a person will make the emotional decision to help you, not for you but because it meets a need for him. That need is the desire for pleasure.

And just what is the pleasure that person will be receiving?

He will get the opportunity to feel important, to feel good about himself.

Why do you think wealthy, successful people often become mentors to young up-'n'-comers they hardly know, don't love or are not even related to? Primarily, because the thrill of the added money or accomplishment is no longer their driving force. They are used to their own success, but becoming a hero in someone else's eyes, sharing in another's success, and simply being helpful for the sake of being helpful and adding to another person's life, all feels really good.

The same goes for this person from whom you're asking for help or advice. It makes him feel so good that he probably will want to help you, and continue to do so.

Of course, it's also important to genuinely appreciate his help and kindness, and to do as much as you can to add value to his life as well.

The Importance of OPS: Other People's Support

In his classic, *The Magic of Thinking Big*, Dr. David Schwartz points out a basic rule for success: "Success depends on the support of other people. The only hurdle between you and what you want to be is the support of others."

If we just replace the phrase "want to be" with the phrase "want to obtain," you can now call this your basic rule for success through the art of persuasion. It now reads, "The only hurdle between you and what you *want to obtain* is the support of others."

In this context, "support" means having people on your side, and this is something you cultivate both immediately and over time through the principles and methods we are discussing.

Matching the Other Person's Words

People rarely argue with themselves. When you can take an idea they have expressed to you and repeat it back to them, they will almost certainly be in agreement with what you just said. This is very powerful. Do it correctly and it will endear you to them—and make them more apt to want to give to you what you want.

This works regardless of whether you are repeating something in that person's own words during your initial conversation, or repeating something in their language from an earlier conversation.

An example comes to mind that took place during the selling process. I had been talking to a manager about doing business with his company, and he went out of his way to provide me with some information for the research I had to do before giving my presentation for him and his supervisor. That courtesy was something he did for all salespeople, and it said a lot about him that he did so.

I happened to meet his supervisor several days later at a local business function, and I related to him that story about the manager's special efforts. The supervisor, being proud of the manager, said to me, "And that wasn't something he *had* to do."

Several months later, about a week before my scheduled presentation, I saw the supervisor again, and when I brought up the effort of the manager, I added the exact words he had used: "...and that wasn't something he *had* to do." I immediately noticed the supervisor acting a lot friendlier and much more open with me.

Here's the fascinating thing about this: I am quite sure he didn't remember saying those exact words to me, but they were words that were comfortable to him, because they were his own phrasing. Consequently, he felt more comfortable talking with me. Why? Because we spoke the same language—literally. By the end of our conversation, he let me know he was looking forward to doing business with me.

It's a good idea to match words, expressions, tone, even volume, in order to speak in the other person's language. Les Giblin says this not only proves you've been listening, but it is also a good way to introduce your own ideas without opposition.

I definitely agree! People are not inclined to argue or disagree with something *they said themselves.*

An Introduction to Neuro-Linguistic Programming

This approach we just looked at, of speaking to people in their own language, has been brought to the forefront as a more specific methodology through the technology of Neuro-Linguistic Programming (NLP). Developed in the early 1970s by Richard Bandler and John Grinder, based on their observations of the relational and conversational techniques of famed psychologists Fritz Perls, Virginia Satir, and Milton Erikson, NLP is a way of quickly and effectively developing rapport with another person.

After reading several books on the subject and taking a private NLP session, I found the approach fascinating and very helpful. In a sense, the example in the previous chapter, of saying another person's exact words back to him, was an example of incorporating NLP. But there's a lot more to it than just that.

NLP teaches us that as human beings, we process information in three different ways, usually with one of them being the primary or preferred channel: *auditory*, by hearing or sound; *visual*, by sight; and *kinesthetic*, by touch or feeling.

Often the words we use tell the listener our primary method of processing information, or at least our mental state at that particular moment. For example, the phrase, "I *see* what you mean," indicates that the speaker primarily processes information in a visual way, or is in a visual mode at the moment. The most effective way to respond is by using similar terminology: "It *looks* good to me, too."

Do you *see* how that response matched the original speaker's state?

If, on the other hand, she says, "That comes across clear as a *bell*," that indicates the auditory, or sound state. If she is mainly kinesthetic (touch or feeling) or is at least presently in that state, she might say, "It just doesn't *feel* right to me," or "I can *feel* it in my gut."

I was talking once with a friend, discussing a personal challenge I was working through, and I said, "It's getting better. I can finally feel the light at the end of the tunnel." Being a student of NLP, she pointed out, "You are kinesthetic, aren't you? You just told me you could *feel* the light at the end of the tunnel! Not *see* the light, but *feel* the light." She was correct.

When you can speak in the other person's language, he is more receptive to you, often unconsciously so. There is even a way to know a person's present state by asking questions and actually watching where their eyes go. It's pretty amazing, and the little bit I've described here is just the tip of the iceberg.

One client tells me he even uses NLP techniques while teaching his Sunday school class. It helps him develop a quicker rapport with his students. There are several good books and classes on the subject of NLP, and I highly recommend learning more about it. It's a great way for you to add some new technology to your persuasion toolkit.

The "I Message"

Here's another principle we all need to internalize, and you'll notice its theme resurfacing often throughout this book. It's called the "I message."

This is not to be confused with being *I oriented*. In *Endless Referrals*, I talk about the idea that when meeting someone new, we need to be *you-oriented* as opposed to *I-oriented*. This means focusing your attention on the other person, investing 99.9 percent of the conversation in asking that person questions about himself and his business. Ask him how to know if someone you're talking to would be a good prospect for *him*.

Being *other-focused* like this is always the best approach to have as you interact with people. It will certainly help in establishing a win/win relationship and mastering the art of persuasion.

The *I message* we're talking about here is something entirely different. This is where we put the onus of a challenge or misunderstanding upon ourselves, which has the effect of taking the other person off the hook, disarming her and making her more receptive to finding a solution to the challenge.

In this sense, a *you message* would mean putting the blame on *her*, which would simply make her defensive and less receptive to a win/win outcome.

Let's say you are in a discussion where the other person is not speaking to you with the appropriate consideration and respect. Now, you might be tempted to say, "Hey, you're talking down to me! You're not showing me any respect here." But this is a classic *you message*, as in, *You are wrong!* Here's how you might frame your response as an *I message*:

"Sam, I feel upset. It might just be how I'm taking it, but it feels as though I'm being put down and not being shown the respect I feel I'm entitled to."

What you've done is put the responsibility on yourself, not on Sam. As a result, Sam doesn't have to react defensively. At the same time, you are still getting your point across loud and clear: the appropriate behavior is not being shown here, and that bothers you.

Let's look at another example.

You're trying to persuade a bank manager to let you cash an out-of-town check without a waiting period. You feel you've been a customer long enough to be given that privilege, but the manager—who has the power to grant your request—is being stubborn and not showing appreciation for your being a loyal customer.

Again, it's tempting to approach the situation with a *you message*: "You're being totally unreasonable here. Can't you appreciate the fact that I've been a loyal customer?" But that just comes across as insulting. Worse, you've also painted her into a corner where it feels to her that if she gives in, she loses. Instead, you can get the same point across in the form of an *I message*: "I really feel that, after years of loyalty to this bank, possibly I'm not appreciated as a customer of value. I've always enjoyed banking here. That might just be my interpretation, but it's very disturbing to me. Could we work this out?"

Diplomacy and tact through an *I message* will usually help you attain the very results you're looking for.

In his book *How to Argue and Win Every Time*, famed attorney Gerry Spence points out the importance of phrasing a statement that ties right into the message. He suggests using the *I message* "I feel upset," as opposed to the *you message* "You upset me." As another example, "I feel sort of cheated" is an *I message*. The *you message* would be, "You cheated me."

Mr. Spence relates how he lets a judge know he feels the judge is not treating him fairly. He'd never do that with a *you message* such as, "You are unfair," or, "You are being rude to me." Instead, he would make his point through an *I message* such as, "Your Honor, I feel helpless," and then go on to explain his plight.

It takes some practice to master the *I message*, but once you do, it will assist you immeasurably.

Defense without Intimidation

The following incident took place at the local county's unemployment compensation department. I was to present the case of a young lady whom I had reason to believe was fired unfairly from her job and whose former employer was contesting her right to collect unemployment compensation. The man I'll refer to here as "the judge" was actually the head of that particular department. His decision would be final. In a sense, he would actually be the judge *and* jury.

Without going into too much detail, I decided to take her "case" for two reasons.

Number one, I was personally familiar with this employer's reputation for dealing unethically with independent contractors and employees. Based on my personal experiences with him, the young lady's story was not particularly hard to believe.

Number two, during the first meeting between the young lady, the judge, and the employer's two representatives—one of whom I knew to be a tough cookie—our young lady (whom I'll call Jill) seemed to have gotten railroaded.

I didn't feel comfortable with that. Jill, who was a friend of a friend, seemed like a sparrow up against a couple of vultures, so Bob "Just Call Me Perry Mason" Burg stepped in.

When Jill came out of that first session all teary-eyed, I didn't realize my friend was going to ask me to represent her, or that this was even allowed, but I did ask her to tell me everything that happened. Jill said the employer's ruthless representative, instead of asking single questions as she was instructed to in order to determine "facts," just kept unleashing accusation after accusation, which the judge did not correct. This intimidated Jill.

Fortunately, before the session's conclusion, the judge suddenly got called to another meeting and had to cut that hearing short and reschedule it. According to Jill, he even suggested she ought to just forget about the whole thing because she didn't have a chance of winning.

Well, we would soon see how the vultures—and the judge—would stand up to the principles and methods of the art of persuasion.

As in any negotiation, I researched all the facts I could, but in this case there wasn't much to go on. According to Jill, she and Karen, the aforementioned office manager, didn't get along. According to Karen, the reason Jill was fired and the reason they were trying to deny her unemployment compensation was that she had done something contrary to the employer's wishes about a year earlier.

What Jill did was clearly wrong. It wasn't public-enemy-crime-number-one wrong, but it was wrong and she shouldn't have done it. She had been soundly admonished for it, and then it—the act—and Jill were forgiven by the owner. Case closed...or it should have been. But over time, some very negative personal feelings, unrelated to the mistake in judgment Jill made and for which she had been forgiven, developed between her and Karen and the employer.

According to Jill, the reason she was fired was the negative personal feelings, and they were fighting her unemployment compensation for no reason other than spite.

With that in mind, I stepped into the office, met the judge, sat next to Jill and across from Karen and her witness, a former coworker of Jill's still working for the employer. With no courtroom experience, I could depend only on the skills we are talking about in this book.

The judge asked if I had any comments or questions before we began, and I told him I did. My plan was to first establish myself to the judge as someone capable of representing a person, because I'm sure he's had many a screamer or arguer come in and try to play big-time lawyer. I also felt the need to politely let him know that I wouldn't accept the intimidation that had apparently happened on the first go-round.

I began by respectfully laying the foundation.

"Mr. Johnson, first allow me to express my appreciation to you in allowing me to represent Ms. Alexander. I believe we can, all of us" (and here I gestured toward the opposition), "provide enough information to allow you to reach a fair and just decision."

That done, it was time to make the "polite, *implied* threat." This is intended to put some fear into the other person's heart, but showing so much respect that he does not lose face and could not be mad at me and therefore want to get even. (There is a whole segment later on exploring the idea of the "polite implied threat.")

"Mr. Johnson," I said, "I'm sure this was simply a misunderstanding, but I feel it must be mentioned. I was made aware by Ms. Alexander that after the first session she was advised to not bother pursuing this issue any further, because the case was already decided. I know that's not true. You would never do that. In this day and age, all that does is get the investigative reporters from the local newspaper interested and none of us needs to be bothered with that."

I could see that he got the point, and he made a point—with his mouth pointed even a little bit more toward the tape recorder he had turned on—that such a thing did *not* happen and never would happen during one of *his* hearings.

I replied, "I knew it wouldn't," implying that I never had any doubts.

Here is a point worth noting: There are times when, in order to get a point across or have someone take action, you must—now here's the key word—*imply* a threat. Never threaten. Simply imply. If you come right out and threaten, you paint the other person into a corner along with his fragile ego. In order to save face, he must argue with you and show you who's boss. That's ego talking, and ego is a big factor in a person's emotional decision to avoid pain. You want to get your point across without making him angry or vengeful. That takes practice, but it's a skill worth perfecting.

Asking Jill the direct questions was fairly easy and straightforward; the challenge came when Karen got her opportunity to cross-examine. Although the judge had advised each of us to ask the witnesses questions and not make statements or give opinions, Karen began to do exactly what Jill said she did last time—loudly voice a tirade of accusations.

This provided me with an opportunity to verbally object, and I did so very politely. "Mr. Johnson, I'm sure Ms. Patterson is not doing this on purpose, but it seems that rather than asking questions—as you had instructed—she's making statements."

He agreed and gently admonished her. She was *not* happy.

A nice break for our side was the fact that she had never before been called on this tendency of hers, and because this was exactly how she felt comfortable expressing herself, she kept doing it again and again—and each time she did, I politely objected:

"Mr. Johnson, I believe that's not a question." And each time the judge, a bit more strongly now, urged her to phrase her questions…as questions! This totally broke Karen's pattern, and she began losing her train of thought.

The one touchy spot was when Karen brought up the incident where Jill was clearly wrong. When it was my turn to reexamine, I reestablished the act and had Jill admit that she knew she had been wrong. In fact, I made no bones about the fact that I agreed—as would anybody—with the fact that she was wrong to have done what she did.

This is a variation of a tactic Abraham Lincoln used as an attorney. He would begin his opening statement by reviewing the opposition's case in a positive way, hitting on a few obvious points that he knew they would bring up anyway and phrasing his statements in such a way that you might think he was actually representing the other party. This established his honesty, integrity, and sense of fair play and justice with the jury.

Do you see what he was doing?

He was saying, "Hey, there are two sides to every story; the other team in this one, they're good people." He was demonstrating—not promising, but tangibly *demonstrating*—that he was going to approach the entire proceedings with fairness and honesty.

Very powerful. And you can apply that, too, whenever you're making your case in virtually any situation.

When applying for a raise, let the boss know, "Hey, I understand where you're coming from. The budget is tough, sales are down, there isn't a lot of discretionary moneys." Right from the beginning, you've established yourself, your understanding of your boss's situation, and your own base of honesty. Now you're in a position to give him or her your side of the story.

When you need to speak to the supervisor or manager of a person who somehow wronged you, resist jumping in with a barrage of accusations against the person. The supervisor gets that all the time. Be more effective by being different.

First, let her know you understand that employee probably has many challenges to deal with during the day, and they are probably just having a bad day today; that you don't blame them personally. I guarantee you that will give you more credibility in the supervisor's mind than a hundred people complaining and being nasty. This is another opportunity to use the three P's: Politeness, Patience, and Persistence. And it *works*.

Back to our case.

I made a definite point of the fact that Jill was wrong, and then I asked if she was fired as a result.

No? Why not?

Oh, I see: your employer forgave you and simply warned you not to make the same mistake again? Ah. And did you make the same mistake again? No, you didn't? And so you were *not* fired for that?

No.

At that point, I at last had the chance to do something that I knew would give me a particular personal thrill, and it did: I added, "No further questions." (I felt like a real *live* television lawyer!)

The rest is somewhat anticlimactic and repetitive regarding how the handling of this situation relates to the persuasion methods we are discussing.

Karen was left at the end with the sole closing argument that Jill had been fired due to the incident in question, and that's why she shouldn't receive unemployment compensation. In my closing, I politely brought up the fact that it had actually been established that was not the case, so, unless another reason could be brought forth, I felt confident that Mr. Johnson "would rule in the way he saw fit."

Notice what I said there: not that he would "rule in our favor," but that he would rule "in the way he saw fit." That gave him credit for being able to make a fair, just, and intelligent decision. It did not come as a complete surprise that, after the hearing was officially over and he had made his ruling, he thanked me for my time.

Oh, yes—he ruled in Jill's favor.

Let the Person Feel It Was His Idea

Would you agree that people are quicker to agree with your point of view if they feel that your point of view is also *their* point of view?

If you're making a point, and it is similar to something the other person said earlier, you can point this out simply by starting out, "And as you pointed out earlier…" and then continuing on with your point. You could also say, "As you were saying earlier…," or, "Joe, as you mentioned…," or, "… as you alluded to," or any number of similar phrases.

But what if the person *hadn't* actually said that earlier?

It really doesn't matter! So long as it isn't contrary to their beliefs, they'll probably relate to it. Just adjust your wording slightly, and you can accomplish much the same effect. Rather than saying, "as you were saying earlier," you can change it to something like, "As you might say, Joe..."

In this instance, you didn't say Joe actually said this, but that it's the kind of thing he *might* say. You're giving him the credit, either for saying it first, or for having that general idea.

I was speaking with the father of a friend of mine. Afterward, my friend said that she noticed how, when I was explaining something to her father, I brought him into the conversation by saying, "As you mentioned earlier, the key is to..." And she said she could tell he was very receptive to that.

I wasn't necessarily trying to *get* something from him, and we weren't debating an issue. We were merely discussing a certain viewpoint that we happened to agree upon. Whenever I can, though, I like to make people feel that they are as much a part of an idea as possible. It's a good habit to develop. It just makes people feel good about the interaction.

Handing Over Power

My friend Debbie had come to visit from California, and due to a mistake she made when checking her luggage, it didn't make it to the airport when I picked her up. She was understandably upset and, since we were leaving on a trip early the next morning, was dismayed to be told that her luggage wouldn't be arriving until after midnight. Since this was not the airline's fault, it would be up to us to come back down to the airport to claim her luggage.

She began to panic and, like most people, was on the verge of both pleading and arguing her case—which wasn't about to do her any good at all. I could see the airline employee already feeling the power of being able to deny her wishes.

Fortunately, I had caught on to this counterproductive transaction early enough to be able to help.

What did I do first? I listened—without *interrupting*—to the employee recite the exact rule stating the airline absolutely did not have to deliver the luggage. It would be arriving at about 3:00 in the morning, early enough to accommodate our departure plans, but not convenient for the airline's delivery person, nor for Debbie.

I agreed with the employee and said that, under the circumstances, I wouldn't blame her a bit for carrying out that rule. What was she going to do, argue with me about *agreeing* with her? No, so now she was disarmed, and her Parent had shifted into a more Adult state of mind.

At this point, I asked her for help while handing the power over to her. (That's important, and I'll review why in a moment.) It went like this, "You know, I'm in kind of a difficult spot. This isn't your problem and it's totally up to you, but I'm wondering if you might be able to lead me in the right direction. We have an early morning trip tomorrow and by the time the airport opens, we should already be gone for hours in order to arrive at our destination on time."

Then I came out with eight key words that will work almost every time. This assumes that you've already done a good job of winning this person over to your side, enough so that they'd *like* to be able to help you. These eight words are:

"If you can't do it, I'll definitely understand."

And then, if appropriate, you can follow them up with these seven words,

"If you could, I'd certainly appreciate it."

Let's review.

First, I gave the power in the situation over completely to the airline employee. This was power she already felt, of course, and that she would have had no matter what—but now, because it was willingly given, she had it without having to fight for it, and that feels totally different. She was shown respect, which is what she wanted. Most people hunger for respect, and I gave it to her without question. Now, she was more receptive to being interested in our problem and a possible solution.

Then came the eight words that would challenge her (nicely!) to show us she had the power to act and be our saving grace.

"If you can't do it, I'll definitely understand." Followed, after a brief pause, by, "If (there's any way) you could, I'd *certainly* (or '*really*') appreciate it." Said with sincerity and a genuine smile.

Communicated with the appropriate combination of humility and sincerity, this will work, assuming there really is a way that person can actually pull it off, either on their own or with the help of someone else.

At approximately 3:00 the next morning, a delivery van pulled up with Debbie's luggage, and the driver personally brought the luggage up to her guest room.

4

The Art of Making People Feel Important

Children Are Often Our Best Teachers

Let's take a time-out from persuasion techniques and learn a lesson on positive, long-term persuasion from a couple of kids.

When dealing with people over a period of time—whether family, friends, associates, or acquaintances—the best persuasion method you can employ is *yourself*. In other words, the essence of you, what you show that person on a consistent, continuous basis. If you show people love, they'll respond to that and want to go out of their way to please you whenever possible.

The following story is from *Parade* magazine's weekly column, "Teens: What Do You Think?" The column's heading this particular week was "Favorite Lines Parents Say. "

Fifteen-year-old Laura Livingston of Florida wrote, "My favorite thing my parents say to me is 'I love you.' Even when I'm mad at them, I love hearing them say it. It's a common phrase in my house, but I feel lucky every time I hear it."

Sixteen-year-old Valerie Sleeter of Virginia wrote, One piece of good advice I got from my father is, "Everyone walks around with an invisible sign around their neck that says 'Make Me Feel Important.'" This was told to him one day by my late grandfather, Colonel Frank Sleeter, in our old country store. I think it is a good example of country wisdom.

Personally, I'd add that it's a good example of country, city, state, and any other kind of wisdom! People want to be around and do things for those people who make them feel loved and important. This is another skill to keep practicing until it becomes an internalized part of who you are.

My guess is that most people don't realize that making people feel loved, valued, and important is a *skill*. But it is, and because it is, you can learn to master it.

Do you know people, perhaps even people you don't really know that well, who simply make you feel *good* whenever you're around them? Don't they make you feel loved, or at least well-liked? Like you are special, important? And don't you want to please these people?

Why is that? You naturally want to please such people for the simple emotional reason of desire for pleasure—in this case, the pleasure of having the opportunity to be around that person more. We all like to feel special and loved.

If it feels good to be around that person, how would you like to *be* that person? You can be. If you internalize the skill of loving people and making them feel important and good about themselves, others will go out of their way to please you.

People give what they get. If you give them love, they'll give it back to you—often magnified. Love people, and the challenge of mastering the art of persuasion will be won before it has even begun!

In a Weak Position? Allow Them to Decide Your Fate—You'll Probably Get the Best Deal

This is another one of those that works most of the time, so long as you've set up the situation correctly and won the person happily over to your side.

Let's say you're negotiating from of a position of weakness, instead of strength. Not exactly the ideal situation. If you read any good book on negotiation, the very first thing it'll tell you is the best way to negotiate is from a position of strength. That strength may be, for example, in terms of having superior knowledge, or having the willingness to "walk away from the deal."

Yet as true as that is, it isn't always feasible—not in the real world.

Let's say you need something repaired on your car. You're in a hurry, or like me, you're mechanically impaired. (I have five left thumbs and know next to nothing about how to fix cars.) Or let's say immediate repair is needed on a part of your home, or you need a copying machine for your office right away.

The best way to handle these situations—since you have the need to take immediate action without the knowledge to negotiate the best price—is to employ the method of simply putting your fate in the other person's hands.

Here's how to do it:

First, let him know how much you believe in him as a human being. Even if you just met him, you can just feel it in your gut and express that:

"Joe, I know absolutely nothing about this particular situation. My ignorance in this area astounds me. I feel comfortable with you, though. I don't know many things, but I happen to be an excellent judge of character. If I'm right about you—and I think I am—you're a successful businessperson who is honest, ethical, and fair. I'd like to just leave it up to you. I know you'll give me the lowest possible price, which will be fair to both of us and will allow me to feel good about referring everyone I know to you."

As far back as I can remember, only one time did I ever feel as though the person I did business with in this way was *not* as fair as he could possibly be. Everyone else has treated me either fairly or better.

What are some of the key ideas we used in that situation?

You showed him respect. You showed belief in him. You know he's fair, ethical, and honest—and said so. People generally act according to the way they feel you *think* they're going to act.

You let him know you respect his business savvy (we all like to feel that we're sharp businesspeople, don't we?) and you wanted and expected him to make a profit. You also mentioned referrals, which handles the "What's in it for me?" factor. You also let him know—very subtly—that if he didn't treat you right, there probably would never be any more business from you, nor any referrals.

You see how that works? In the blink of an eye, you can go from being at a great disadvantage to being treated fairly—and possibly even superbly.

Negotiation and the Art of Persuasion

Let's talk about negotiation for a moment.

One could quite correctly say this entire book is about negotiation. Let's face it: any time we want something from someone, whether it's money, an act of kindness, respect, or anything else, we are negotiating. More and more books these days are being written on win/win negotiating skills. I like that, and I've learned a great deal from many of them.

Pick up any one of those books or audios and you'll receive lots of practical tips for becoming a much better persuader. I know that whenever I'm involved in a negotiation, I find myself employing many of the principles, strategies, and tactics we're discussing in this book.

Yes, it's all negotiation, in one form or another. And just learning the information in this book will put you way ahead in terms of negotiation skills.

Still, I encourage you to pick up some negotiation-specific books and audios. Attend a negotiation class or course.

You'll learn some very simply techniques you can use to help you further your persuasion abilities.

You'll also be introduced to some of the negotiation tricks that skilled negotiators might one day (or already do) use *against* you. Why is that important to know? Because ignorance, at least in the context, is anything *but* bliss. What you don't know can absolutely harm you, financially and in other ways.

While you'll never use manipulative or harmful tricks against others, you will benefit greatly by others not being able to use them against *you*!

Declining an Offer the Right Way Sets You up for a Win

The following story hits on an interesting point, once again dealing with showing respect—especially in a situation where many people wouldn't.

When you're involved in a negotiation and a person offers you a deal that you are simply not interested in, remain respectful no matter what. By declining an offer respectfully, you're positioned to receive "a benefit of a miscommunication."

Often companies buy a large quantity of my audio program entitled *How to Cultivate a Network of Endless Referrals*, to be used either as resale items or as continuing training tools for their salespeople. One particular company's representative asked me if they could make a duplicate of the recording master and produce the audios themselves. They would then give me a royalty per program sold. They asked this because my program retailed at a higher price than they were willing to pay. He was, in other words, asking if it would be okay with me if he *pirated* my program!

Talk about an offer that I *could* refuse. There was no way I'd ever agree to an arrangement like that. But instead of bluntly turning him down, or saying something like, "Are you kidding! I'd have to be crazy to agree to something like that! What do you take me for, an idiot?" which would have offended him, embarrassed him, and hurt his ego, I was careful to decline in a very respectful manner. I said, "Mr. Sanders, I appreciate your kind offer, and I feel honored you'd want to share my information, but if I did that, it would be unfair to all the people who distribute these and get such a substantial discount for doing so."

He looked very surprised.

Not surprised that I declined his offer—but because he didn't realize I gave distributors and quantity buyers such a major discount. He'd never thought to ask, and I had just figured he knew. I was wrong: he didn't! When I told him the discounted price, he was delighted, and we agreed on the transaction right there. He became a good client.

Had I put him down while turning him down, which would have been a natural impulse, because what he was proposing was almost insulting—do you think we would have ever gotten to the point of understanding? Even if we had, would offending him have helped or hurt my chances of our coming to an agreement?

Declining an offer respectfully will dramatically increase your chances of finding agreement, if or when one can possibly be found.

Many times, after telling a prospective client what I charge for a speaking engagement, I have been talked to as if I were committing highway robbery. I've actually been laughed at! "Ha! You're kidding! I'd *never* pay a speaker *that* much!"

Hey, I have an ego, too, and when someone talks to me like that, I remain polite, but I sure don't offer to discuss any other type of arrangement. While I don't lower or discount my price as a matter of principle (and of practicality), there are often other options that I *could* come up with, including referring them to speakers I know who can provide great value but who charge a lower fee. But if they laugh in my face, am I thinking of various options that might solve their problem? No, I'm thinking that I don't like being laughed at.

However, if they say, "Bob, I'd love to have you come in for us, but I just couldn't possibly pay you that kind of money," that's completely different. We still might not be able to work anything out, but maybe we would. Possibly we could restructure my fee with a trade-out for one of their company's products, or design a combination of a fee with guaranteed or advance book sales. And again, I would at least go out of my way to find them another speaker who would do them well at a lower fee level, and under such circumstances, I have often done just that.

This holds true for circumstances large and small. If someone is simply asking for a small favor, a quick phone call, a moment of your time, but it's something that just isn't possible for you at the moment, the same principle applies.

Whatever the situation, when you need to decline, it's important to do so with respect and make the other person feel good about herself. When you do, if there is any chance for a productive outcome, you've just greatly increased the odds that this will happen.

Get the Person from Whom You Want Help Involved in the Challenge

People will be more apt to help you solve a challenge if they feel your challenge is also their challenge.

Les Giblin raises this point beautifully in *How to Have Confidence and Power in Dealing with People*. He suggests that instead of asking someone to help you with your challenge, make it his challenge as well simply by asking him how he would solve the problem.

For instance, you're trying to figure out how to connect a gidger-gadget. You know that Tom has good mechanical skills and it would be a snap for him to make the connection. You, on the other hand, are like me and cannot successfully assemble a two-piece Fisher-Price® tool that says, "Snap on here."

You could just come right out and ask Tom to do this for you, but unless he's a good friend or just a naturally helpful guy, chances are good he'll find a reason to decline. But what happens if you say, "Tom, you're a master with your hands, and I'm the worst—how would you suggest I begin to put together a gidger-gadget?" Tom, whose ego you just fed quite nicely (you just called him a master, remember?), will probably want to show you how to get started. And he might not stop until he's done.

Let's say you're trying to get an introduction to Deborah Durham, the decision-maker of a company who could use your products. You're sure that if you could just get in to see Ms. Durham, you could have her as a very lucrative, long-term client. You know a man in the company named Steve who personally knows Ms. Durham, but you don't quite know him well enough for him necessarily to want to go out of his way for you.

Instead of simply asking him to make the introduction for you, what if you got him personally involved in the process?

"Hi, Steve—hey, could I ask you for a piece of advice regarding a certain challenge I'm having?"

You've made Steve feel important, and that's good for his ego, which might cause him to be interested in how he could attain that particular pay-off of emotional pleasure.

"Sure," says Steve, "what can I do for you?"

"Well," you reply, "if you don't mind my asking, if you were an outside salesperson who needed to see Deborah Durham at your company in order to show her your products, and you just couldn't get past her secretary, what would you do? I can't figure it out."

Wow, what a challenge you've given Steve! How could a person given so much respect for his inside knowledge possibly refuse to share that information? Not that it couldn't happen, mind you, but you've certainly increased your odds of receiving the introduction you desire.

Another win!

How to Disagree and Still Win without Intimidation

No one likes to be corrected, even when they say something that is absolutely incorrect.

Your prospect tells you he would never buy your product because it doesn't have the capacity to cross-file data to the 102nd mega-degree. You know that's not true: it actually *does* have that capacity. But if you come right out and tell him he's wrong, he'll resent you for it.

You could convince him logically of the fact that your product not only can cross-file data to the 102nd mega-degree (whatever that means), but could also do it at the speed of light, while blindfolded—and the chances are your prospect will still say "no." He'll find a way to say "no" to protect his position anyway he has to, because he feels his ego has been bruised.

Would you agree with that? At least nine times out of ten—right? We've all seen it happen.

Your boss gives you back a report you handed in and asks you to correct one area that you know was right. You researched it, checked and double checked it, and you know *it's right*. How do you suppose your boss will respond, though, if you simply tell her that she's wrong, and your report is right? Is there a slight chance that her ego may not wholeheartedly appreciate your pointing that out? Is there just a tiny chance, in fact, that she'll still somehow find a way to make both it and you *wrong*, either right now or in your next report?

There is more than a tiny chance that she'll do that: there is a humongous chance. Unless this person is an extraordinary human being, you bet she will!

Instead, phrase your disagreement in a way she can live with and even appreciate. Take the onus off her and put it on your own "lack of understanding." This works like a charm.

When having to disagree with another person's statement in order to get your point across and get what you want, it's often best to lead into the correction with statements such as, "Correct me if I'm wrong..." or, "I don't understand..." or, "Could you clarify something for me...?"

Pat tells you he can't deliver your new furniture by Friday. You could *react* by saying, "You did it the same day for Dave Sprazinski on a special delivery order!" Instead, why not *respond* with, "Joe, correct me if I'm wrong—you know these things much better than I do—weren't you able to get my friend Dave Sprazinski's furniture to him in on some sort of, I don't know, special delivery order?"

Marjorie says, "I don't like how that looks in this particular order." Two days earlier, that's exactly the order she said she wanted it in, and changing it now would cost you a whole lot of time and money. But if you come right out and tell her that, she probably won't budge an inch.

Why not lead into your statement with, "Marjorie, could you clarify something for me, because I want you to be totally happy with my order. I interpreted what you said to look this way. It really does work great, too, your judgment was right on the mark. Can we review this step by step?"

Keep in mind, when you have to correct someone who is wrong, you need to do so without offending them and their ego. Use diplomatic phrases that allow you to *tactfully* move into the information you need to express in order to get agreement from that person.

Long-Term Persuasion through Personalized, Handwritten Thank-You Notes

Here is a simple method for creating consistent, long-term success with people. This suggestion may at first seem like it's a bit of an inconvenience, but you'll quickly find that it really isn't inconvenient at all. And once you develop this success habit, it will make a world of difference in your ability to persuade. You'll have people on your side *for life* after you do this one thing, and challenges that might otherwise have come to the fore may never actually surface.

What is this amazingly simple, powerful secret to long-term success? The habit of writing thank-you notes.

I know, we've all been taught to do this. Our Moms made us write thank-you notes after attending a birthday party, or eating dinner over at someone's home, or every time we got a gift. If you're in a selling-related field, you may have learned about thank-you notes all over again in Basic Sales Training 101. However, for all we've been taught about how we should write thank-you notes, very few people actually write them! And they don't realize that they are missing a golden opportunity.

By the way, I'm *not* talking about "thank-you emails" here. I'm talking about actual thank-you notes, written on paper and sent through the mail. While saying "thank you" by email is also an excellent tool when used appropriately, it is *not* very effective for what we are discussing here.

When you send a personalized, handwritten note, you are remembered for a good reason: you have distinguished yourself from all those who don't send such notes—which includes practically *everyone*.

I've found sending thank-you notes to be one of the most (if not *the* most) powerful tools in building a huge and effective network, both professionally and socially. I've also noticed that people with the most impressive networks are avid note-writers. Does that say something? I think it does.

Not only will you be remembered—and very favorably—by the person to whom you sent the note, you will also be remembered for having cared enough to make the effort. Show someone they matter to you, and you will matter to them.

When the air-conditioning repair person comes out to fix your unit, send her a nice, handwritten thank-you note (a thank-you note to her boss wouldn't be a bad idea either). If you ever need them in an emergency, there's a good chance they'll remember you and your note and come through for you.

When you've had a particularly good meal at a restaurant, drop a nice handwritten note to both the waitperson and the owner or manager. You'll most likely be treated as a VIP forever after. I can tell you, both from personal experience and the experiences of others, this works *big time*.

If for whatever reason you ever need help from a police officer, be sure and send him a thank-you note, and while you're at it, one to his commanding officer, too. You certainly want them on your side in the event of (heaven forbid) a real emergency.

I repeat, both from personal experience and the experiences of others, this works *big time*.

After you meet a person who may be in a position to either purchase your products or services or refer you to others who can, send a nice, handwritten note. When salespeople do this with consistency (consistency being the key), they receive dramatic long-term and even short-term results.

I suggest making your note card 8½ by 3½ inches, which fits nicely inside a standard #10 business envelope, and on 60- or 70-pound card stock. (This is heavier than regular 20-pound bond, but not as heavy as a postcard.) The card's design could have your company logo on the upper right hand side and, below that, your picture, which will help the recipient remember who you are. The picture should be small and professional according to the image you wish to project. (A lot of people are embarrassed at first to include their picture, but it really does help others to remember you. There is much truth to the saying, *out of sight, out of mind*.) Below the picture you would typically place your address and phone number.

I suggest also putting your brief benefit statement across the bottom. For example, a financial advisor might use, "We help people create and manage wealth."

Don't let your information take up too much space on the card. You want this to be a note oriented toward the other person, not an advertisement for you, which would have exactly the opposite effect from what you want. Regardless of the business you're in, or even if you're not in any particular business at all, you can set the card up following the basic structure just described, but geared to your own unique situation.

If you'd like to see a sample of mine you can use as a basic model, visit www.burg.com/notecard. You'll notice mine has a picture of several of my books at the top and no benefit statement across the bottom: in my case, the books are my positioning message. Set yours up in the way that will work best for you. Again, though, please remember, it is not a "sales piece." It's a relationship-builder. If you make it salesy, you'll totally defeat the purpose.

When writing the note, I suggest using a pen with blue ink. Blue ink has been proven to be more effective, both in business and personally.

Regarding the envelope, *handwrite* the person's name and address (again, with blue ink) and make it a point to *hand-stamp* the envelope, rather than putting it through a postage meter. You want the letter to be opened, not to be perceived as junk mail.

Anyone in the business of mail order will confirm that letters that look personal on the outside increase their odds of being opened tenfold.

The note itself should be kept short, simple, and sweet. For example:

> Pat, Thank you so much for the super job you did with our air conditioner. It's great to know of a service professional who really understands the meaning of "service." I'll let all our friends know about you.
>
> Thanks!
> Tom

Do you think the comfort of you and your family will take precedence in the future? You can bet on it!

When meeting a potential business contact, your note might read,

> Hi, Ann, Thank you. It was a pleasure meeting you at the Chamber function. If I can ever refer business your way, I certainly will.
>
> Best regards,
> Debby

When you write a nice note to the waiter and owner of the restaurant, how quickly do you think they'll respond next time to make sure you and your family are seated at the best table and are served a delicious meal? The answer: very quickly. The same goes for practically anyone to whom you send one of these handwritten notes. It's one of the best methods ever for developing that feeling of *know, like, and trust* toward you.

These Notecards Can Even Turn Enemies into Friends

Here's an example of how to turn a potential lemon into a lemonade using these notes.

At an annual convention of an association to which I belong, I was sitting at a table with about ten other people. There were several conversations taking place simultaneously around the table, and without realizing it, I was talking louder than I should have been.

A man sitting next to me—an older gentleman and a true center of influence within the association—turned to me with a touch of annoyance in his voice and said, "Bob, you seem to have quite an audience there."

He could have been more tactful in his reproach, but his point was made—and taken. And he was absolutely right.

Upon returning from the convention, I immediately sent him a personal note. Not an apology note, but a thank-you note. It read:

> Dear Mr. Jones, Thank you. It was a pleasure meeting you at the recent convention. Best of success in the coming year.
>
> > Regards,
> > Bob.

That was it. Nothing was mentioned about the incident. It was just a simple thank-you note.

Did it achieve the desired result? Well, at the following convention one year later, upon spotting me, Mr. Jones (not his real name, of course) made his way over from across the room to shake hands and greet me like an old friend. A good relationship developed, and he and I are very friendly to this day.

Concerning the timing of when you send your note, my suggestion is simple: do it *right away*. In many communities, if you mail a letter before midnight, it will arrive locally the very next day. Having it appear on a person's desk at work or in their home the day after they met you or performed a service for you is a very nice touch.

I suggest developing the habit of sending these notes immediately. One major factor that separates those who succeed in any area of life from those who don't is the ability to take action at the correct moment. In today's super-fast-paced society, that moment is *now*.

Actually, *ability* isn't even the correct word. The more accurate term is *self-discipline*.

I believe the following holds true: The longer you wait to do what you know you should do now, the greater the chances are that you'll never actually get around to doing it. This is known as the Law of Diminishing Intent.

And sending these notes is too important to never actually get around to doing it.

5

Everything Is Negotiable

It's Not Negotiable? Sure It Is!

Every time you seek to get something from someone that he was otherwise not about to give, even if it's just that person's momentary cooperation, you are negotiating. Different situations call for different tactics.

One challenge might be when the other person has some power and enjoys using it as much as possible in order to satisfy his ego. In this situation, we'll again utilize the three P's—politeness, patience, and persistence, and we'll also *give* that person the power he already has anyway.

I was in Toledo, Ohio, a few hours before I was to speak at a large sales rally. The tables were being set up where people would have the opportunity to purchase my books and audios after I'd finished speaking. One important aspect of merchandising after a program is having the tables set up in a prime space. As people exit to the restrooms or the concession stands or to stretch their legs in the hallway, they'll be close enough to the table to remind them of the merchandise for sale. They can see the CDs, DVDs, and books, pick them up and browse them, and be more likely to purchase them.

So the positioning of our table is always very important. Obviously, though, it is much more important to my staff and me than it is to the convention arena personnel. Understandably so: they just want to see things run smoothly, with no major hassles that would make them work even harder than they already have to.

Surveying our Toledo site, we noticed that our table was further away from the main door then was beneficial, so we had the table moved to a more advantageous spot. Since the space right next to the door was already taken, the spot we chose was against a wall directly opposite the door. This was actually even better. People would be facing us directly whenever they left the main room and would almost bump right into us upon reentering. In fact, I wondered, why hadn't any of the other speakers, entertainers, or exhibitors thought of that?

I soon found the answer. Mr. Anderson, one of the arena officials, quickly made his way over to our table and informed us we'd have to move. "You can't set up there," he declared. He was most definitely poised for a knock-down, drag-out argument.

I didn't blame him. No doubt he has at least one of those tussles for every program held at his arena. A bitter argument ensues, and then the person ends up moving, leaving both parties angry and resentful.

Well, he wasn't going to get *either* of those from me as far as I was concerned: no argument—and no moved table.

The first step I took, as you would have guessed by now, was to consciously make the decision to respond, not react. *Respond, not react.*

I extended my hand and said, "I'm Bob Burg." He took my hand and gave it a handshake (what was he going to do, refuse?) and told me his name was Scott Anderson. He was just a bit disarmed now and a little nicer as he continued, "You're going to have to remove the table, and set it up down the hall. It's against the rules for a table to be set up here—and unfortunately it's non-negotiable."

"Oh, I understand that," I replied.

I continued, respectfully using his title, "Mr. Anderson, what could we do to work out a special arrangement—setting up down the hall will absolutely kill my sales, and I'm wondering if you could use your influence in making a special exception?"

What I just did was to affirm in his mind the fact that I respected him and the power he had. By using the phrase "special exception," I was helping him to think of an answer that he could use *and* take credit for, too.

However, it wouldn't be quite *that* easy. This was going to take some patience and persistence. "There *is* no special exception," he replied. "As I said, Mr. Burg, there is no negotiating on this."

"Oh, I agree," I replied.

I learned the power of agreement from a very successful entrepreneur by the name of Tim Foley. A former All-Pro football player with the Miami Dolphins, he has made a fortune in the business world, one reason being that he has incredible skill with people, diplomacy being his forte.

Rumor has it that Tim reads the book *How to Win Friends and Influence People* every few months in order to keep his skills sharp in that area. I'd say that is excellent advice. He also works hard, is consistent in his efforts, and is a real giver of himself to others. That's a sure recipe for both business and personal success.

"Oh, I agree," I told Mr. Anderson. "Obviously there's a reason for this rule. It must be a protection of some kind, but you know what, I can't figure out what it is—I only know that if I don't have this space, I'm in big trouble. I can tell you're the type of person who seeks solutions to challenges—do you have any advice on how we could pull this off?"

He was getting a bit flustered now for a couple of reasons. For one thing, I wasn't giving up. That probably wasn't so strange; I'm sure he was used to exhibitors violently arguing with him for the longest time. The difference here was that he was getting an argument. Just a totally respectful guy massaging his ego, while gently challenging his wisdom and expertise by asking him to come up with a solution.

"The problem is, Mr. Burg, with your tables here, it's still too close to the door. With your materials and books set up before the program starts, people will be crowding around your table to shop. It will make it hard for people wanting to get in and get seats to get past the crowd. That's why, unfortunately, as much as I'd like to help, it's still non-negotiable."

Ah—finally, good news, I thought to myself.

You might be thinking, Bob, are you crazy?! He just gave you awful news! Nnnoooo, he didn't. He just supplied me with the answer—an answer that would allow him to let us stay there, while emotionally satisfying him and logically giving him the loophole he needed so he wouldn't stop from doing the right thing just for the sake of protecting his ego.

You may have noticed that he talked about the challenge being people crowding around the table *before* the program, not allowing the rush of people wanting to take their seats to get by. But we *never* open our table up for transactions before the program. We've found sales are significantly better by not opening it until after I've presented my program on stage. At that point, people have significantly more interest in checking out the materials at the table.

The challenge Mr. Anderson was describing, in other words, *would never happen.*

Of course, that's *logically* true—but his ego, like anyone's, would not readily make decisions based on logic. So I phrased it to him this way:

"Mr. Anderson, you just came up with the answer! I will give you my word that we will not open up the table until *after* I speak on stage. In fact, we'll cover it right now with these sheets over here, so no one will even be able to see anything—and it won't have any impact at all on the crowd coming in. You figured out the solution we needed—and I can certainly live with not opening my table until *after* my presentation is over."

It worked. He got the credit, and I got the solution.

The positioning of the table was about the best I've ever had.

We had one of our best sales nights ever.

Here's the truly funny part: In order to save face and his power position even more, he made us agree to one additional provision—we had to promise that the next morning, we would set up in our original spot. Now, this made absolutely no logical sense. None at all. The only challenge with our being in the spot we wanted was the opening crowd needing to get to their seats, and that had been worked out. By the following morning, the problem would be history. But his ego needed that concession from me in front of everyone else, apparently, to make sure we all knew he was still the boss.

And that was just fine with me. I knew he was the boss, and I also knew that tomorrow didn't matter. The majority of business is done immediately after my live presentation. By the next morning, those who still wanted my materials would easily find my table twenty yards away from where we were right now. They weren't the ones who needed it right in front of them. So I "grudgingly" agreed and we had our spot.

I figured that by the next morning, he would have forgotten all about the final concession, since his point was made. But guess what? The next morning, sure enough, our table had been moved back to its original position!

So I ask you: do people make decisions logically or emotionally?

Remember the three P's—*politeness* (which is also *respect*), *patience*, and *persistence*. Let the other person feel their power, let them want to help you, and let them think the solution was theirs. If necessary, concede a minor point to make them feel you didn't totally get what you wanted.

Sometimes, losing a little bit of nothing is a very worthwhile tradeoff to come out ahead.

How You Ask Is Often More Important than What You Ask

Sitting at the Denny's restaurant counter for breakfast, I noticed the waitress possessed one of the most unusual foreign accents I'd ever heard. It was very nice, just different. In fact, I could hear that the couple next to me were trying to figure out its origin—as was I. When the waitress came back over to our general area I said, "Excuse me, that's a lovely accent you have. Where are you originally from?" With a big smile, she thanked me, and mentioned that a lot of people seem to enjoy her accent.

As she walked away, the husband of the couple next to me said to his wife, "Now *that's* how you ask a person something."

I believe he was saying that taking a moment to phrase a question nicely—with kindness and respect—and saying it with the right intonation, makes a big difference in getting what we want and need from people. I simply call it *the art of persuasion.* (And by the way, you can imagine the special service and attention and smiles I received from the waitress for the remainder of the meal.)

A wonderful speaker and author by the name of Glenna Salisbury tells a very funny story that truly illustrates the fact that, while the words we use are important, they often aren't nearly as important as the way we say them.

Glenna tells of a young English teacher who had worked hard all year trying to help an Asian transfer student master the English language. Understandably, he was very appreciative. On the final day of school, the teacher walked into her classroom and on her desk was a single yellow rose. Next to it was a note written by the young man. It read:

> Dear Teacher, one day this rose will fade and die, but you will smell forever!

The words may not have been exactly right, but do you think she felt insulted or complimented? She was delighted, because of the young man's intention.

Here's a little exercise I learned from Zig Ziglar that demonstrates how the way you say something can dramatically alter what you mean to say. In this exercise, I want you to accentuate the one word in the sentences below that appears in *italics*. Just put extra emphasis on that one word as you read out loud. Each sentence is composed of exactly the same words—but watch what happens when you place emphasis in different places.

I didn't say she stole the money.

I *didn't* say she stole the money.

I didn't *say* she stole the money.

I didn't say *she* stole the money.

I didn't say she *stole* the money.

I didn't say she stole the *money*.

Aren't the differences interesting? All because you merely accentuated a different word in the exact same sentence!

Yes, it isn't what we say, but how we say it! Our pets know what we mean by the way, tone, and manner we talk to them. So do our children. It's safe to say your customers, prospects, loved ones, friends, and anyone with whom you may need to win over can sense the very same thing.

Smiling Equals Success

Read any good book on people skills and there will be at least a mention of the power of a smile. It's also the easiest technique to learn in order to master the art of persuasion.

For some people, smiling takes a bit of practice. (Hey, for some it takes a *lot* of practice.) We're not talking about a smile just to be positive, although that in and of itself is certainly a good enough reason. In fact, let's discuss that just a bit.

It's been said, "You don't smile because you're happy— you're happy *because* you smile."

That's true! It's a physiological fact. When you smile, there is a chemical response within the body that actually compels you to feel happy.

Do this: smile really big, right now, and try and feel sad...

Can't do it—won't work. When you smile, you make yourself happy, improve your attitude, and also improve the other person's attitude and expectations of you.

John Mason, author of *Let Go of Whatever Makes You Stop*, says, "One of the single most powerful things you can do to influence others is to smile at them."

Very true! Dale Carnegie devoted an entire segment of his great book, *How To Win Friends & Influence People*, to this single fact.

While my smile is genuine, I also know it is one of my most effective tools when transacting with others.

Very few people smile without a particular reason. Thus, by smiling, you give yourself a distinct advantage over everyone who is not smiling. Get that sincere smile on your face—and do it before you deal with the service person, the bureaucrat, your boss, the waitperson, your spouse, anybody. Get yourself ready for that person to like you and smile *back* at you!

I employ this simple action all the time, every day, with amazing results, and I know others who do the same. They quite often get waited on or helped at a crowded desk first, just because the person sees them with that smile.

We spoke earlier about having to talk to a manager regarding a challenge. Or, you might have to question someone about the fact there's an extra charge on your bill. Greet that person with a really nice smile and watch their mindset shift to match yours.

The person who smiles becomes a pleasure to deal with.

Smile...

When walking into a restaurant on your way to take your seat, whomever's eyes happen to meet yours, *smile* at them. Do that enough and people will notice you. In fact, they'll describe you as the one with charisma.

I stop at my local Dunkin' Donuts every morning to pick up coffee. As I walk up to order, one of the employees or another patron who's seen me in there before will comment on the fact that I'm always smiling. In fact, I do this practically everywhere I go.

Recently, one said, "You're the only person I know who's in a good mood in the morning." Once an employee said, "Gee, you're in a good mood today." I responded with a smile, "Have you ever seen me not in a good mood?" He replied, "Actually, no I haven't."

Do you think I get good service and smiles from the employees and other patrons? Sure I do. If I ever needed to approach anyone there for any specific reason, do you think I'd be taken seriously? Absolutely!

The truth is, I am *not* necessarily always in a good mood. I have my difficulties, challenges, and frustrations, just like everyone else. But that doesn't mean I have to wear it on my face in public and spread my bad mood to everybody else.

If I'm depressed or hurting inside, that's nobody else's business. What's that old saying? "Half the people don't care that you're feeling bad—and the other half are glad about it." I'd like to think that's not entirely true, but the point is that people do respond more positively to those who appear to be positive.

The fastest way I know to change my bad feeling is to smile. A smile causes the release of neurochemicals called endorphins into your brain, where they are responsible for the positive mood human we call *joy*. That means you can change how you feel by simply smiling. (And notice if *that* makes you smile...)

When you smile, people begin talking about you in a positive way. What's the payoff for that? You probably won't know exactly what it is until it happens, but the general result, in both short and long term, is that you make others feel good and you contribute positively to your world and the world of others.

Does it work for you in the business world, too? Sure, because you never know who you're going to meet and who will take notice of you. A smile makes people curious about you. *Why is he smiling? What makes her so happy?* They may inquire about what line of work you're in and ask about you personally. It's happened to me.

What about on a social level? The same. Smiling makes you more attractive to others. And I don't mean necessarily in the physical sense—though it's true there, as well.

My Dad has been a master of the smile from as early as I can remember. People would see him coming and practically roll out the red carpet, whether it was the first or the twentieth time they had seen him. I was always amazed. Still am to this day. I've never met anyone else so loved.

You know some people who are like that, don't you? It's sincere! They like people and they show it. Even if you have to work at making it sincere, you can do it. It pays well. *Really* well. Keep practicing and you'll love the results so much, it will *become* sincere. As Dr. David Schwartz said in, *The Magic of Thinking Big,* "Action precedes feeling."

One of the best examples of the power of a smile I've ever experienced took place many years ago when I walked into a bank in Tampa, Florida. There were three lines at the tellers' windows, and I noticed that one of the lines was quite long while the other two were short. Why, I wondered, weren't the people at the very end of that long line moving over to join one of the shorter lines?

As soon as I caught a glimpse of the teller who was serving the long line, I understood why. She had the most incredible, radiant, friendly smile I've ever seen, before or since. Her smile was worth waiting in as long a line as it took, just to have the chance to bask in the glow of that smile one-on-one, even if for just a few moments. I'm not usually overly dramatic, but hers was a smile that obviously intoxicated a lot of people in a very positive way.

I took my place at the end of the line and waited with everyone else... and I had just come in to ask for road directions!

We like to be around people like that because they make us feel so darn good. I was not born with a smile like that bank teller's; I had to *learn* how to do that. Perhaps you feel you have to learn how, as well. The great news is that it doesn't matter whether or not it comes naturally for you: you *can* learn to master this skill.

Les Giblin suggests, that in the same way voice instructors teach their pupils to breathe deeply and let their voices come from way down low in their bellies, we must do the same with our smile. Instead of smiling from the diaphragm, smile from deep in your heart. You have to smile from deep in your heart, if you want it to have real impact. A plastered-on smile that goes only skin deep won't have much effect. We've all seen people with that kind of smile, and it just comes across as phony, insincere, or manipulative. Your smile *must* be genuine, or it won't have all these positively persuasive results.

Practice your smile constantly. Put yourself into a happy state by first by thinking of something very pleasant. The more you practice, the more your friendly, persuasive smile will come across as—and *be*—authentic, natural, and *yours*.

Getting People to Give You More

You can easily persuade someone to give you more than she normally would. Simply plant the seeds with the person as she is doing what she'd normally do.

For instance, imagine you love hot carrots as a vegetable with your meal. You're at a cafeteria and the server is beginning to spoon the carrots onto your plate. You want more than you know she is planning to give you. You've already greeted her with a smile, which sets you apart from everyone else and she's taken notice—she smiled back. As she begins to serve the first spoonful you say, "Umm, thank you, I love those." You'll get more carrots than most customers, even if that server is not usually inclined to break routine.

Tell the mechanic working on your car, "John, you're an *artist*, man, the way you work on these things." People love being called *artists* at jobs not usually associated with art. He'll probably give you the best service he's capable of giving.

A friend of mine used to refer to the man making the submarine sandwiches at our favorite sandwich shop as an *artist*, and he was. He loved showing off his artistic sandwich-making skills to my friend and me. Of course, that took lots of extra meat and fixings, as well as extra care and attention.

To the busy woman in the clothing store who's loaded with people wanting her attention, smile and say, "I can tell you're busy, and I don't want to be a pest, I'll try and take up as little of your time as possible." Chances are you'll get more of her time than will the next hundred people.

"I Know That You . . ."

As people of ego, you and I don't appreciate being told by someone what to say or not to say, what to do or not to do. Even worse is for someone to instruct us in something *we already think we know all about*.

When you need to be sure that a person will come through for you, you must phrase what you say in such a way that he and his ego will not be offended. Tell him that you know that *he already knows*.

Before giving the specific instructions, you might (with genuinely encouraging tone) begin with the words, "I know that you..." and then provide him with the necessary information.

Here's an example: "Tom, *I know that you* believe in being sensitive to people's feelings; that's why I have no doubt you'll go out of your way to be especially tactful when telling Dave about the mistake he made on that report."

"Rhonda, *I know you already know* that the statistics need to be filed in a three-tier setup. You have a way of always putting these things together correctly."

"Marie, *I know you were going to* stack these here anyway; I just needed to tell you because of my own insecurity."

Saying things that way takes the sting out of it, leaves people feeling good about you—and about *themselves*—and assures that they, in fact, *do* what's expected of them.

The Same Thing Over and Over

My former neighbor Carol, a staff supervisor for a local mid-size company, called to invite me to a local dinner theater show. As a holiday bonus, her company had decided to send the entire staff to the theater for a night of fine food and entertainment, and Carol invited me to come along as her guest.

When we reached the theater that evening, the person with the tickets had not yet arrived, so the manager would not let us into the main dining area to sit down and begin eating. He politely asked us to wait at the bar. Nursing a soft drink, I sat and waited with the rest of them. Carol, who could be somewhat fiery and argumentative at times, wasn't about to let it go at that.

She announced to us all that she was not happy. She wanted us to begin eating right away so that we'd have plenty of time to enjoy our food. As far as Carol was concerned, the manager knew we were simply waiting for the person with the tickets to arrive, so why couldn't we just go in now! Although I happened to be in agreement with Carol, I was an invited guest and didn't feel it was my place to say anything.

Then Carol announced, for all of us to hear, "I'm going to raise a fuss about this!" And she did.

After calling the manager over she began to verbally assault his intelligence, or lack thereof. How do you suppose he reacted? The fact that I used the word "reacted," and not "responded," probably gives you a hint. He argued right back at her.

This went on for several minutes, with Carol telling him why he should let us go in and the manager telling us why he couldn't. A totally emotional conversation between two adults, neither of whom were acting as adults. There was Carol, acting the Parent, admonishing the manager as if he were a Child, and the manager, feeling scolded, slipping perfectly into that Child role and defensively fighting back.

Seeing that this was not going to end anytime soon and realizing how simple it could be to solve, I waited until the two combatants took a simultaneous breath—and at that moment, seeing my opportunity, I said to the manager, "Sir, I totally understand where you're coming from and what the challenge is. In fact, in a similar situation, I might feel the same way. Let me ask, if we were to assume total responsibility for the seating assignments—if I could get the staff supervisor herself to agree that you would be totally off the hook—would you consider letting us go in now?"

He looked at me with a smile, and to everyone else's amazement (though not to mine!) he said that wouldn't be a problem. "Great!" I replied "Because being able to eat our meal without having to hurry would certainly add to our enjoyment of the show. By the way, I appreciate your help and understanding."

He responded—yes, *responded*—by saying, "My pleasure."

He then personally escorted us to our seats and checked on our comfort several times throughout the evening. At one point later in the evening, when he noticed that one of the people in our group got up with her camera to take a group picture, he even walked over and offered to take the picture for her, so the woman with the camera could be part of the shot.

Carol was astounded by what took place and asked what my *secret* was. I explained it really wasn't so much a secret as much as a genuine caring for others and, a desire to find a win.

I'm not sure whether she grasped the concept or continued to go through her life fighting a never-ending battle. A lot of people do that. The more we share these principles and methods with others, however, the more, little by little, we can do our part to make this an easier world in which to live.

Building Rapport: A Key to Effective Persuasion

People generally respond well to people who are like them. Having similarities with another person increases your chances of persuading her to go along with your ideas. Often, however, you find that you are really nothing like that other person. At first thought, it doesn't seem like the two of you have *anything* in common.

In such cases you need to really stretch. What can you find that you *do* share in common with that person?

Are you both married? Do you both have kids? Do you both have kids about the same age? Are you weekend athletes? Sports fans? Have similar hobbies, pleasures, recreation?

How do you find out? Through asking questions.

Geographical sameness can be determined fairly easily, and that's a good start. Ask where she lives. Ask where she grew up. If you both live in Massachusetts, but are originally from Boston, that's a great starting point. You can bring up similar areas you're both familiar with. If you live in Florida, and she lives in Louisiana, but both grew up in different towns in Massachusetts, "Hey, I'm originally from Massachusetts myself." That's something you can build on in establishing rapport with that person. You can *really* stretch it. Let's say you live in Florida, and she lives in California. You grew up in Maine, and she grew up in New Jersey. "Hey, I'm from the East Coast, too."

You can stretch one pretty far, say, up until you get to the point of saying, "Hey, I'm from that planet, too." Geographic origins or location, as well as other similarities, can be utilized as excellent rapport builders.

Pretend All the Other Drivers Are Your Next-Door Neighbors

Two concepts mentioned throughout this book are *politeness* and *responding* as opposed to *reacting*. If you are not used to regularly enlisting these two key principles, then you'll often get caught in what I call *the heat of the moment*.

This is when the challenge with another person occurs, and, because we haven't yet internalized in our minds and hearts the ideal way of handling the situation, we slip up and lose control. The situation (and often the other person) ends up controlling you, instead of you controlling the situation.

Here's an exercise that will serve as excellent practice in self-mastery in the heat of the moment:

Ever notice when you're in a car, the other drivers seem to take liberties they might not take if they were not under the protection of a one-and-a-half-ton moving vehicle? People can be rude. They'll butt in line. They'll cut you off. They'll even give you the "I'm Number One" sign with the incorrect finger in the air.

In his book *If Life Is a Balancing Act, Why Am I So Darn Clumsy?* Dick Biggs suggests pretending that all the other drivers are your next door neighbors.

Isn't that brilliant?

And you can use that great idea in working on your skills of politeness and responding. Every time that another driver is rude in any way—no matter how much you have to fight yourself at first—*respond* by being polite. Give them a wave or a smile, or nod your head in acknowledgment, or even put your hand up as if to say, "Sorry, my fault." You can also let a driver go first at an intersection, or let them cut in front of you from another lane.

You'll be amazed at how many people will be friendly in return (often to their own surprise and bewilderment), which is a good feeling. You'll turn a potential enemy into a friend. You'll develop your skills of politeness, and responding *instead* of reacting, in record time. That's an all-around win!

By pretending that all the other drivers on the road are your next door neighbors, you'll begin internalizing for later action these very important skills for mastering the art of persuasion.

One Result of Being Impolite

The following example will probably happen only rarely, but people who succeed generally base their success on those little differences that are not noticed nor acted on by the masses of average, less successful people.

One afternoon as I was walking out my office door, I crossed paths with a young, sharply dressed man. I politely smiled and said, "Hello," as I would to anybody, yet he responded with what I call a "don't bother me, buddy" look. He had obviously figured I was *just* another salesperson, or one of my company's employees. He probably didn't guess I *was* the company. When I got to my car I called Ilene, my office manager, and asked who that was.

She explained that he was the guy we were buying the two new computers from and that he was outside her office now waiting for her. I told her what happened and said I'd rather not buy from him, and that if she'd like, I'd come in and tell him personally so she wouldn't have to. No, she said, she would be happy to handle it herself—the last time he had called, this same young man had been rude to her on the phone. He had called to ask for directions, and Ilene happened to pick up the phone instead of the receptionist. The man was quick and hurried as she providing him with the directions, and as soon as she finished, he abruptly hung up without a "Thank you" or even a "goodbye." I'm guessing he thought it was okay to act that way to a *mere* receptionist.

That young man lost two nice, easy sales that day— about $5,000 worth. He thought the sale was in the bag, and was just coming in with the paperwork for us to sign. We had already ordered the computers over the phone—a situation some people in the selling profession call a "laydown." The sale could not have been any easier for him. He had to really work at losing that one ... and he did.

I guess you could say it's a good idea to be polite to everyone you meet. Not only is it simply the best way to act, but also, you don't always know who you're talking to.

As a kicker to this story, several months later I found out that an acquaintance of mine had gone to work as manager of that computer store. I related what happened and he was not at all surprised. He explained that the three salespeople that had been there when he started—the *gentleman* from the above story being one—had created a whole bunch of ill will for the company by treating practically all their prospects and customers in a similar fashion.

They were all let go, fired when the owners heard enough of the negative feedback from customers (and *former* customers). My acquaintance added that he and a couple others had in fact been brought in by the ownership to restore the goodwill that had once been an integral part of their company.

Politeness, Respect, and the Implied Threat

After days of not having our repeated calls returned by our sales representative, my office manager took the only reasonable course of action she could and called the man's boss to ask why that was. Ilene handled this perfectly, first letting the boss know that we've always been pleased with their company and the excellent service they've provided to that point.

We soon received a call from the sales rep, Gary, who had just taken over the area, and he was understandably not at all happy to have been "told on." He and I had never met before, but he asked to speak with me.

I was happy to take his call. "Good morning, Gary," I said.

Gary began with a really defensive edge to his voice. "Why did you call my boss instead of calling me directly?"

"Unfortunately, Gary, we've had a challenge with our equipment for the past couple of days. We called you several times, and, surprisingly, didn't hear back from you."

Gary replied, "I just took over this territory and I have other customers. I can't get back to everybody right away."

I responded, "I appreciate that. I know you're very busy, but a call of acknowledgment would have made us feel a lot better and then we could have scheduled an appointment for you to come in."

Despite my politeness and respect, he still wasn't grasping the idea. He again replied that he was busy and could only return calls, in the order they came in, *after* the jobs were done.

Now came what is referred to as the nice but *implied* threat.

"Gary, I understand where you're coming from and sense that right now you're feeling a lot of pressure from people within your new territory. Here's where I am: We need to know we can be serviced by whatever company we choose to do business with. I'd like it to remain yours. You and I will obviously have to work according to each other's needs and expectations, and if we can't, we'll both have to do what will be best for our individual situations."

He understood.

You know what I was doing without an explanation: establishing a foundation of politeness and respect. I then built our position in the sales representative's mind as a customer worth maintaining.

Remember, people deal with ranters and ravers and screamers all day long. If they are going to have to sacrifice one of them or a customer who is polite and respectful, which one do you think it will be?

When courtesy alone didn't get through to Gary, it was time for *the nice but implied threat.* It was effective in letting him know not to confuse my being nice with being weak. The implied threat is so effective because it clearly communicates credibility and seriousness of purpose, yet it doesn't paint the person into a corner from which he can't escape without his ego screaming in pain. And, if you simply issue an overt threat without making sure you frame it in a nice way—if, for example, I had just said, "Listen, Gary, either you answer our calls right away, our we're taking our business somewhere else!"—then that's exactly what you do: you paint the other person into a corner where he either has to fight you back, or give in a resent you for it ... which will translate in the long run into poor service anyway!

Okay, then, but why, you may wonder, did I go through all that trouble instead of just changing companies right then and there?

Well, let's take a look at the results of that conversation.

Gary began popping in to check on us whenever he was in the area. One time, when we were short-handed and had to process a bunch of orders—which had nothing to do with *his* company—Gary actually insisted on staying and helping us. Unbelievable! I think Gary paid us so much attention because we were probably one of the only customers that treated *him* so well.

So back to the question: what if I had simply changed companies? Who knows how *their* rep would have treated us? Or the next, or the next after that? Eventually, we might have even gotten back around to Gary's company, and we'd have had zero credibility, since we'd be doing business with them out of weakness, not strength. And how about all the time lost for setup and the expense it would have taken to switch companies?

No, the best way is to handle it right the first time—and have *everyone* come out a winner.

6

How to Deal
with Difficult People

Don't Try to Teach a Pig to Sing

Is there ever a time when what we are discussing just won't work? Yes, there is. When is that, you ask? Let me explain it this way:

I once heard the saying, "Don't try to teach a pig to sing. It will only frustrate you, and really annoy the pig!" Likewise, you could say, "Don't ever argue with a crazy person."

When I use the word "crazy," I'm not talking about one who has a medically determined condition beyond their control. I'm talking about people who have taken on an entire personality of disagreeableness or have a particular—and usually particularly negative—attitude about something.

These are the people, who for whatever reason just aren't going to work with you, me, or anyone else. Their emotional state has predetermined the facts, and their mind cannot be opened through logic nor emotion. Their position is, "I already know what I think—don't confuse me with the facts!" They probably feel wronged by someone or something that has nothing to do with you, and now they're giving back as good as they got.

Mind you, such people often have no idea that this is what they're doing. They always seem to believe they are the most understanding, open-minded people in the world. They're not, of course—but neither you nor I are going to change their minds about that.

We all have encountered at least one person like this, and as much as it goes against the very grain of our thinking, we need to let them go and do their own thing.

This is only a very last resort, of course, but it is one of those rare times when one has to simply say, "Next!" If you try and persuade someone has determined that they are unpersuadable, you'll only frustrate yourself, and really annoy them!

The Pre-Apology Approach

As I walked up to the ticket counter, I noticed that the agent did not look happy. In fact, he looked downright miserable. Not a good sign. I needed him to be working *with* me, because I had to change a couple of items on my ticket. But it was clear that this was a man who was prepared to be difficult.

How do you work effectively with that potential challenge and win *without* intimidation?

I approached with a smile and a friendly greeting—which had absolutely no discernible effect. I have to admit, at this point, I was starting to feel like telling him, "Hey, shape up and get with it!" But that would have just turned a potential enemy into an *actual* enemy. Instead, I disarmed him by using what I call the pre-apology approach: I apologized in advance for everything he was *going* to do for me.

Here's what that looked like:

I'm sorry you've got to bother with all this stuff, it must be a real pain in the neck.

That was it. It was that simple.

From that point on, he went above and beyond for me. All he needed was for someone to understand what he was feeling. Can you believe it? With that one small statement, his attitude completely changed for the better. I'll bet he was friendlier for the customers following me, too.

The natural reaction would've been to match his scowl and battle to an eventual lose/lose. My associate, who was with me at the counter, compared me to her former boss, saying that he would have screamed and yelled...and *maybe* gotten his way, but maybe not, and in either case, would have ruined the moment for everyone involved, and quite possibly the entire day.

Remember Simeon ben Zoma's saying, "A mighty person is one who can control his emotions and make of an enemy a friend."

What, Who, and How

While reading a very good book by Milo O. Frank entitled *How to Get Your Point Across in 30 Seconds or Less*, I was reminded that there are three essentials for every form of spoken or written communication: "Know *what* you want, know *who* can give it to you, and know *how* to get it."

Know exactly *what* it is you want from the transaction with the other person. Focus your efforts on an outcome you'll be happy with.

Know *who* can give it to you. Do you need to find a tactful way of moving from the person you're now transacting with to the person who really has the power to say yes? Nearly anyone on any level can say no. You need to know who it is who can help you obtain what you want.

You accomplish the *how* part by using the skills and methods in this book, along with those you learn from other sources as well.

Find the Who

Years ago, in an issue of *Selling* magazine, I read about a gentleman by the name of Joe Cousineau. Now president of his own company, he expertly used the art of "finding the who" when he was regional sales manager for another company within the industry.

Cousineau was trying to land an account with the largest purchaser in his region—a company already doing huge business with his competitor. He arrived right on time for his meeting with the purchasing agent, but was then distressed by the treatment he received.

The purchasing agent did not invite Joe to come in to make his presentation, but instead, while standing in the lobby and looking at his watch, told him he had exactly five minutes to explain why the company should change over to Joe's product, instead of staying with the supplier already in use.

Joe knew that five minutes was far from enough time, and to make matters worse, the purchasing agent never made eye contact, showed no interest in what Joe was saying, and would check the time every thirty seconds. At the end of five minutes, the purchasing agent abruptly stopped the presentation, announced time was up, shook Joe's hand, turned on his heel and left.

Joe was stunned. The receptionist, who witnessed this transaction, was quite embarrassed by her boss's behavior but was not in a position to do anything about it. Joe left. Had he not been taken by surprise and hundreds of miles from home, Cousineau probably wouldn't even have given a presentation. He would have most likely questioned the purchasing agent as to how they could work out a better time to meet in a more efficient setting.

The way he handled the situation from that point on was a textbook example of "finding the who" and then winning without intimidation.

After returning to his own office and reassessing the situation, Joe realized that he did not deserve that kind of treatment. Furthermore, he decided, it would also be wrong to let that purchasing agent's rude, unprofessional attitude keep the man's company from realizing the benefits of Cousineau's products.

Joe determined that the "who" to talk to was the president of the company—which was his next call.

Once he had the company president on the phone, Joe explained that his product had been proven to be superior and outperform its competition at far better terms and prices, and that he had arranged a meeting earlier in the week with the company's purchasing agent to review those points.

Then he calmly explained to the president what had transpired and told him that the purchasing agent's conduct—now this is a *great* word—*confused* him. What an excellent way to frame the situation! By doing so, he put the onus of the misunderstanding upon himself—a classic *I message*—which you *know* had to have piqued the president's curiosity.

He then continued by saying that he had decided, before closing the books on this company altogether, to break the usual chain of command and phone the president directly. He told the man that he was new in the territory, and asked if it was in fact company policy to give vendors only five minutes in the lobby for presentations. If not, did they have a special arrangement with another supplier, and was that possibly the reason for his unusual treatment?

"Was the purpose to discourage me?" Joe phrased that question carefully enough to not imply any improprieties between the company and their present supplier.

The president asked Joe to describe again precisely what happened and if there were any witnesses. After learning about the receptionist, the president then went and confirmed Joe's story, then came back and apologized—and gave Joe an appointment with him personally, *without* the purchasing agent present.

Cousineau put together a transaction which to this day ranks as that division's third-largest account ever. It was also the sale which Cousineau credits for turning his career around. As for the purchasing agent, management decided to put him into sales, so he would learn what it's like to get the sort of mistreatment he had been dispensing to others.

Joe Cousineau's story provides an excellent example of "finding the who," putting that person on your side, and then expertly *winning without intimidation*.

How to End a Telephone Conversation Politely

When someone, maybe even a close friend or associate, is constantly calling and keeping you on the phone, how do you end the conversation politely and effectively without offending that person?

Here's what works for me and for others, too: cut the call off by interrupting—only by interrupting *yourself*.

How? Like this:

Begin the conversation with, "Hey, great to hear from you, I'm just about to… (step out, meet with a client, move on to a phone appointment, etc.), but I've got about thirty seconds, what's going on?"

The person may not be sensitive or aware enough to end in thirty seconds, even though you've tactfully told him. That's okay, though: you've already set the call up with those parameters, so you have in essence given yourself permission to cut it short without being rude. When you reach the point where you really feel you need to go, wait until he finishes his current point, then start responding to him— and after saying a few words, cut *yourself* off: "Oh, so sorry, I forgot—I have to run to my… (call, meeting, skydiving appointment, radical surgery—whatever). Nice talking with you, though. We'll talk again soon."

That will set you free—politely, and promptly!

Making the Best Out of Being Around Someone You Don't Like

Hey, we're all human, and because we are, there are likely to be certain people we just don't like being around. It happens! It may be someone whose personality style grates on your nerves. Often, it's appropriate to simply avoid that person. Other times, though, that's not going to be so easy. For example, you may be thrown together in work or some special project. Or—and this is perhaps the worst-case scenario—the person you don't like is related to someone close to you, maybe your best friend's wife or your boss's husband.

The best way to handle the situation is to work on helping that other person adjust their style—without emotional attachment to the results. To train them, without their realizing they're being trained, to do things in a more positive and likeable way.

Just make a game out of it. Not at their expense, mind you; have fun *with* them—the two of you *together*. Catch them doing something right, or even make up something you wish they would do right and then compliment them on doing it (even if they haven't done it yet). Build on small successes. They'll begin to continue doing those things they get verbally rewarded for. Whether positive or negative, behavior that gets rewarded, gets repeated.

Understand, of course, that depending upon that person, this shift may not happen quickly at all, and will thus take a good deal of patience (yours) to follow. Sometimes, it will not happen at all. And when it doesn't, that's where the non-attachment comes in.

You might need to simply accept that what is, is, and that a growth experience is now taking place.

Edification

To edify, according to one of the meanings in *Webster's*, is *to build*. When you edify a person, you literally build them up in the minds of other people and, perhaps most importantly, in their own mind as well.

Edify a person, to others and to themselves, even for the things you *wish* they would do. They'll soon begin to believe their own press, and start adopting the traits and behaviors for which they are being edified.

All of the following could be statements that, while perhaps not entirely true at the moment are being said, could certainly become true—especially after the person gets this positive feedback:

"Jim sure is precise in the way he fills out his reports."

"Mary, I love how you always handle people with such perfect tact."

"My spouse is the most supportive partner in the world."

"Dave, one thing about you—you may be direct, but you are always fair."

When in doubt as to what to say *about* someone or *to* someone—*edify!*

Resolving Conflicts

One of the most difficult challenges for human beings is resolving conflicts. There will be times of anger and frustration with others no matter what the relationship—friend, spouse, parent, child, coworker. It's one of those life things that happen even when we do our best to avoid them.

How do we resolve these conflicts and repair our relationships? How do we return to speaking terms and mutual enjoyment?

Dr. Paul W. Swets, author of the wonderful book *The Art of Talking so that People Will Listen,* discusses what he calls Conflict Resolution. According to Dr. Swets, "Once discord has set in, talk is difficult. In fact, discord may have resulted from talk—sharing hostile feelings or dogmatic opinions. Yet talk also can be the best remedy when it is directed by four distinct purposes and their corresponding messages."

These four purposes and their respective messages are:

PURPOSE MESSAGE

1) Define the problem   "I hear"

2) Look for agreement   "I agree"

3) Understand feelings   "I understand"

4) State views calmly   "I think"

Dr. Swets explains that we need first to identify the problem or challenge. Are you sure that both of you are upset about the same thing? Many of us have found ourselves involved in a conflict with someone only to later realize that it was simply and literally a misunderstanding. "She thought I said *this*, but what I really meant was *that*."

That's why Dr. Swets's corresponding message to defining the problem is, "I hear." "What I hear you saying is…" Dr. Swets suggests making sure that you have stated the point to the other person's satisfaction before moving on to the next step.

That next step is to look for agreement. Find something within your challenge upon which you both agree. Take it upon yourself to proactively find that point of agreement with the other person. Express the message, "I agree." "I agree that I said some unkind things."

As mentioned earlier in the book, finding agreement with the other person's viewpoint will lessen their defense mechanism. They will find the situation less threatening and be more inclined to see your point. Once there is agreement, the foundation is established for the next step.

Step three is understanding the other person's feelings. We've covered the fact that everyone likes to be understood. Dr. Swets would say, "I understand that you might feel…" completing the sentence with a word that describes what you think the other person is feeling. Dr. Swets provides a list of words to fit various situations:

Afraid	Angry	Anxious	Confident
Defensive	Depressed	Happy	Hurt
Troubled	Uncertain	Upset	Worried

The good news is that even just giving the message that you understand is a positive step. It shows the other person that you want to understand. According to Dr. Swets, "If you misinterpret the correct feeling, [the other person] will tell you. When you state it accurately, you establish one additional powerful source for dissolving discord, because most people desperately want to be understood at the level of their feelings."

The fourth and final step is to state your views calmly and follow with the corresponding message. Start with "I think…" or "The way I see it is…" Complete the sentence with your opinion. Dr. Swets suggests doing this as calmly and briefly as possible. His example is, "I think that you ignored our prior agreement." Another message might be, "I think we need to keep our lines of communication open."

Dr. Swets makes one point in particular which truly fits the philosophy of winning without intimidation: "When the Conflict Resolution model is employed, the focus of the controversy gradually changes from attacking one another to attacking a mutual problem and solving it."

I appreciate the wisdom Dr. Swets has shared in his excellent book, and highly recommend you add it to your persuasion tool kit.

The One Minute Manager Knows

If you have ever read that great classic, *The One Minute Manager*, by Drs. Ken Blanchard and Spencer Johnson, you'll remember that one of their most famous pieces of advice for leaders or managers in effectively dealing with their employees was, "Catch them in the act of doing something right."

When you catch someone in the act of doing the right thing, make sure you verbally acknowledge it and them, and, if appropriate, make sure everyone else in the office or home or whatever the circumstance may be knows about the recognition as well.

Isn't it great to catch a child in the act of doing something right, and verbally reward her for that? Adults thrive under that kind of positive attention every bit as much as kids do.

When the customer service person handles the person in front of you with patience and consideration, make sure you let them know you noticed, and how impressed with them you are. If there are others around, it wouldn't hurt to lavish your praise in a voice loud enough for them to hear, as well.

Once again, whether positive or negative, behavior that gets rewarded gets repeated.

How to Write a Request to Get Action and Get What You Want

People are not always quick to take the action necessary to live up to their responsibilities. At one time or another, we've all had to chase people for money they owed us and promised to pay but never got around to doing it, or something similar. Then there are those who never planned to pay at all.

You write a nice letter of request. It doesn't get answered. You write another. Again, no answer. You begin to write more sternly, then threateningly—and it goes downhill from there.

It's actually much easier and more cost-effective to write one letter that gets the result you want. In the following scenario I'll show you just one example. There are many.

I believe the idea will come through as to what really works. Not that it will work every time and with every person. Some people are just the type who live life by not fulfilling their obligations. Typically, though, this *will* work if the person has even a reasonable amount of pride, self-respect, and conscience. Fortunately, that describes most people.

I had shot a commercial for a production company, and that evening I discovered that sometime during the day of taping, a suit, two shirts, and several of my ties mysteriously disappeared. There was a slight chance that the other spokesperson involved had taken them by mistake, which could easily be determined, but the odds of that were slim.

The company and I disagreed on whose responsibility it was to protect my suits from the fate of "permanent borrowing." After some discussion, we agreed that if the other spokesperson did not have them, the company and I would each assume equal responsibility. They would send me a check for half the amount it would take to replace the clothes right away. It turned out that the spokesman did not have the clothes.

The person at the company who was my liaison to the owners seemed to be rather slow in sending the check. Hoping to do further business with that company, I didn't want to offend them by nagging for payment.

After a couple of months, my feelings began to change. My liaison wasn't returning my calls, and that really bothered me. Not returning my phone calls is a sure way to get my goat. To me, it's a sign of disrespect. The issue truly wasn't the money. Suits can be replaced. Not a big deal. It was, in fact, *the principle of the thing.* They are a good company, comprised of people I very much enjoyed knowing and working with, and I felt they had reneged on a promise. Maybe this is my old-fashioned thinking, but a promise *is* a promise.

I sent the following letter, incorporating many of the principles we are discussing. It focused on respect for the other person and invited them to do the right thing while allowing them to save face. (So that the company involved in this example cannot possibly be recognized, I've altered the names and some of the details. The content, however, is totally representative of the situation and my letter.)

Dear Mr. Renfro,

It was a pleasure meeting you during the commercials we did for Company X. I appreciate the opportunity to work with your company and the professionalism your firm exhibited.

It is with regret that I must bring up an issue I would have hoped to have been resolved months ago, and I won't assume you are even aware of the situation. May I explain?

On the evening of our shoot it was discovered that one of my suits, two shirts, and several ties had been inadvertently taken by someone during the day's taping. There was an extra suit left, however, which we assumed belonged to Mr. Ken Matlin, the other spokesperson. John, my liaison, and I thought that possibly Ken mistakenly took my suit and left me with his, as he had to leave in a hurry during the afternoon to catch a flight. I promised to send the suit to Ken, which I did immediately upon returning to Florida. Unfortunately, Ken did not have my suit, so no one ever found out what in fact had happened.

Although over the following months I often reminded John of this challenge, he was vague in his response as to my requests for payment. Throughout the planning and taping of the commercial, John had been wonderful to work with, a true professional, so I'm sure that the vagueness of his responses was because, despite trying diligently, he had not been able to coordinate all parties necessary.

I reminded John several times that I would be willing to go 50/50 with your company on the reimbursement for the missing clothing. (Although I don't feel that guarding my clothes during taping should have been my responsibility, I was still—and still am—willing to split the cost.)

Unfortunately, although I have continued to leave messages both on his voice mail and with Diane, his assistant, I'm now finding that, to my surprise, John is not even returning my calls.

Can we work this challenge out to our mutual satisfaction? I hope you feel, as do I, that the best situation is that of the win/win variety. I will hope to hear from you soon. Please feel free to call me at 1-555-1212 or email me at bob@burg.com.

Thank you for your consideration.

Bob Burg

If you enjoyed the way that was handled, you might want to reread the letter a few times, just to pick out the underlying principles and how they played out in the wording of the various points it made. You'll probably note how his company was complimented, his sense of fair play and honor was well acknowledged, yet how what I wanted from them was still made quite clear. Even John the liaison, who really is a good guy, was treated very well, though I definitely let the boss know about his not returning my calls. (That really *is* a big bugaboo with me.)

How did the letter work?

The very next day, at 10:30 am, Federal Express delivered my check.

Handling Threats by Phone and Clearing Up Credit Challenges

Many years ago, a woman who was working for me related a challenge she was having. Apparently, the owners of a startup company she went to work for a year or so earlier had asked her to put her name on their cellular phone application. Although most of us would wonder why an employer would make such a request, and immediately suspect something wrong, Sue, in good faith, did them this courtesy.

As you might expect, they turned out to be less than honorable, and when they went out of business soon after, they left her stuck with a $1,500 phone bill. Sue explained the situation to the cellular phone company, but they insisted that the responsibility for the phone bill was hers and hers alone. They were not concerned at all about the men who owned the company who did not honor their obligation.

In other words, "it wasn't their problem."

Knowing her as I did, I could easily believe that Sue did not make the story up.

Over the course of the year, she would get bills and pay as much as she could. She was not in great shape financially, however, and soon began getting collection letters from the phone company. Finally, a man claiming to be the head of collections called and told her to pay the bill in full or he would have the local sheriff subpoena her to appear in court. According to this man, she would then have to explain to the judge why she wasn't honoring her debt.

Sue asked me to help her out, which I was only too happy to do.

First, I called the company to see if a simple explanation of the predicament might be enough to have them call off the dogs. Although the service woman with whom I spoke was very understanding and sympathetic (in fact, she explained that many secretaries had been victimized by that same scam), there was nothing she could do about it, and the bill would have to be paid. Apparently, the man who called Sue earlier was the man who made that decision. I thanked her very much for her time and understanding and asked to speak to Mr. Gregory.

I introduced myself as Sue's employer and explained that she was a victim. Would the company he worked for be willing to write this off or even reduce her debt? Well, he came on a little strong with me, of course, because that's just how he's used to operating. He said he would need all the money now, or he would send the sheriff of our county to visit Sue with the subpoena. I guess the sheriff thing is his usual vehicle of threat.

I replied, "I appreciate your wanting to bring this to closure right away. Since Sue doesn't have the money and you know you can't get blood from a stone, why don't we do this: I will write you out a company check for $400 if, at that point, you'll drop the entire issue. Naturally, I need to have a signed letter from you stating that to be our agreement."

As you already know, what I was doing was, with politeness and respect, establishing with him that he was now dealing with someone he wasn't going to be able to bully, but someone who would still work with him. (After all, I didn't blame the company for wanting their money—and I was even willing to help out in order to get Sue off the hook.) His initial threat and tone I simply ignored. While it would have been natural to have reacted to that, it wouldn't have been productive. Instead, I'd let my actions help bring forth a mutually beneficial conclusion.

The $400 I offered him was way below what he would be willing to settle for, and I knew that, but I wanted to see where he was. One rule of negotiation is to shoot as low as you can because, first of all, you never know, you just might get it. Secondly, he might come back with another offer. And if he'll come down once, there's a really good shot he'll come down again.

He said, "If you'll make it $1200 and send me a certified check, we'll call it even."

I replied, "Oh, thank you for your offer, I appreciate it… Unfortunately, I'd have to decline that, because it's still way too much money. In fact, I know that you know Sue was coerced into putting her name on the agreement, even though it was her employer that took the service. Her former employer apparently has some challenge with ethics. Maybe you should go after him; it might be a little easier to collect the money from him."

Mr. Gregory replied, "That's not our policy."

I responded by saying, "I appreciate that. You know, Mr. Gregory, it's not my policy to pay even a portion of my employee's former employer's cellular phone bills, either, but I'll stretch a bit if you will. I'll tell you what; let me think on this for a day and I'll call you back tomorrow. Thank you so much for your time, I know you want to work this out to everyone's benefit and I appreciate that."

I called my lawyer and asked him what to expect. He told me this guy was "no different from any other collections person and would bully whomever was easiest." Note: certainly not every collections professional does this. Unfortunately, because of those who do, the industry has been saddled with that reputation. Most collection agencies adhere to proper guidelines and go about their job in a legal and ethical manner. He probably could get the money, but he'd have to decide if the effort and money involved was worth it. Also the time, since he was more than three hours outside of our county.

Mr. Gregory called before I did, but he asked to speak to Sue. The receptionist had been instructed to transfer his call to me if that happened (call it a hunch), and I answered, ignoring his indiscretion.

"Hi Mr. Gregory, Bob Burg, how are you?"

"Uh, fine, Mr. Burg. I came up with a decision. Send me a check for $900 and we'll close this account."

I'm thinking, where did this guy come up with the figure $900? A better tactic would have been something like $937. A number like that gives the perception of a specific reason; it suggests that calculations of various costs and other factors had to have been involved . An even number like $900 suggests it was a number grabbed out of thin air. (Which I'm sure is exactly what it was.) It didn't matter now, though. He should have taken my original offer of $400, which definitely *was* a number grabbed out of thin air.

"Mr. Gregory, again, thank you so much for your time. I appreciate your win/win attitude. Here's what I think we should do."

Now, let's pause so I can explain that what I'm going to do right here is a combination of the technique I call the implied threat, together with a common negotiating technique called the "higher authority."

You've heard me use the implied threat before. That's when we very nicely, without painting the person into a defensive corner where his ego is at stake, let him know that if he doesn't accommodate, there will be unpleasant consequences. An example of this might be (in a pleasant, sincere voice), "Bill, I've enjoyed doing business with you for so long and would like to continue to do so—I'd hate to feel as though my business isn't worth the extra whatchamacallit I'm asking for." You didn't *actually* threaten, but your intent was made clear.

With the *higher authority* technique, you give your power or authority to make the final decision up to someone else, either someone of a higher position in your company, family, etc., or someone of greater knowledge. For instance, "I can't possibly make a decision on that without consulting with my lawyer." Or, "Let me run your offer past my (wife, brother-in-law, business partner, choose anyone else you can think of) and I'll let you know."

There are several benefits to this—one being that you can always come back with another offer without coming off as the bad guy. Not to mention, the person with whom you're negotiating is put in a position of never exactly knowing where your side stands.

Neither of these two methods is ideal, but at times, especially when they will keep you from being taken advantage of by a less than ethical person, they are appropriate.

Back to our conversation with Mr. Gregory: let's hear how the combination of these methods sounds.

"Mr. Gregory, again, thank you so much for your time. I appreciate your win/win attitude. Here's what I think we should do. After consulting with my company lawyer, who certainly knows a lot more about the law than I do, he suggested very strongly my not paying any of this bill, and suggested the same for Sue. You represent a fine company with an excellent reputation. The fact is, we all know that the people who ran up the bill should be the people responsible for paying the bill. Here's what I will do for you:

"I'll give you my lawyer's phone number. He said he'll be delighted to speak with you. Unfortunately, Mr. Gregory, he doesn't have the win/win attitude you and I have. He's one of these guys who'd rather fight than work things out as gentlemen, as you and I believe in doing. Man, I've seen him tie things up, write letters to company presidents, the Better Business Bureau, newspapers, and so forth.

"Frankly, he can be a real pain. But you might enjoy speaking with him and finding out where he stands on this issue. I'll call him for you if you like and ask him to call you right now."

Mr. Gregory told me that wouldn't be necessary—he'd get with him himself if he felt he needed to.

Sue received a letter from the company shortly after informing her that the approximately $1,500 she owed had been removed from their computers.

I cannot stress enough that the art of persuasion, if applied correctly and persistently, will come through for you more times than not.

Frankly, I'd have been more than willing to pay the $400 I originally offered, just to help Sue out. Instead, it worked out so that Sue was let off the hook—and I didn't have to pay a dime.

Making Up Is (Not Necessarily) Hard to Do

There are times when you might need to break the chain of command to get to the person who can make a major purchase of your products, and your successful sale may make your first contact resentful. However, it still behooves you to befriend that first person, because she could still play an important role in your relationship with that company.

Letting a person save face after you've gone over her head—and won—can play a major role in how smoothly your relationship with this new client or customer will proceed. The next time you see or talk to her, thank her for her help or contribution in getting the sale.

"Frank, I really appreciate your help," or, "Mary, I appreciate your support and look forward to working with you over the next few months." That's all you need to say.

I know, Mary had absolutely nothing to do with your successful sale. You're right. She knows that. You know that. And she *knows* that you know that. However, by letting her save face, you are protecting her ego, showing yourself as a classy and trustworthy person, and giving her good reason to work harder to help you from that point on.

In my experience, that person will be on your side with loyalty that's truly an asset.

The only instance in which this will not work is the one that goes back to something we spoke of earlier: "You can't argue with a crazy person." If the other person is irrational and totally offended by your actions, he probably won't come over to your side—at least not right away. You'll just have to make sure your other relationships within that organization are even stronger so there's no way sabotage can come into play.

Usually that will not be a challenge. Letting that person save face after you've gone over their head and won will generally bring them over to your side.

The Eight Magic Words that Will Practically Always Get You What You Want

I had changed my flight on the phone the night before. The operator assured me that she had waived the $75 fee for changing the tickets, but the woman at the counter the next afternoon told a different story.

I didn't want to react by arguing, yelling, and demanding. Not only would that not have helped, but my bags might have been rerouted to Tahiti...and I was heading home to Florida!

I needed to respond by staying cool and thinking before speaking.

"I'm sure I misunderstood," I *admitted*. "The person on the phone was very helpful. Although she did assure me I wouldn't be charged that money, I realize it's put you in a difficult spot, and I apologize for that." Upon hearing that, the agent at the counter started to relax, becoming more friendly.

Then I said what I call the *eight magic words* that—assuming you've been kind and polite—will generally prompt a person to pull out all stops in order to help you:

If you can't do it, I'll definitely understand.

After pausing a few seconds, I followed with, "If you can, I'd certainly appreciate it." If you feel it's appropriate, you might even add the words, "I don't want you to get yourself in hot water over it."

After checking her computer, she responded, "I'll do it for you this time."

Treat people with proper respect. Understand their concerns and challenges. Make the request to let them know what you want them to do. Use the eight magic words: "If you can't do it, I'll definitely understand." Win *without* intimidation.

A desk agent at my local airport always tries to wait on me, because he knows with me he's always in a safe place. He's with a person who shows respect and seems to understand what he's going through.

Not surprisingly, *he always* comes through for *me*.

7

The Art of
Persuasion in Action

Back to the Implied (But Nice) Threat

There are times we need to let the person know we mean business, and aim to be satisfied in our quest for whatever it is we need or want.

I was speaking at a corporate conference on the topic of Business Networking and Creating Endless Referrals, and near the end of the talk, I shared some of the principles and methodologies we're discussing in this book. Little did I know they'd be applied so quickly by one couple in the audience. The very next day, a husband and wife gave me the following account:

While attending the conference, Mr. and Mrs. Michelson had a small amount of jewelry taken from their hotel room. When they called the manager, he was at first standoffish and told them to just "file a report."

Mr. Michelson, who had just come out of my seminar, very calmly replied, "You know, I could do that, and I thank you for your suggestion. Actually, I was really hoping to leave your hotel's name out of it. I'm part of a 2,000-person convention, and we're supposed to report anything like this to our meeting planner. It really makes me uncomfortable to bring your hotel's name up, though, because up until now, we've really enjoyed our stay."

Although I don't know all the particulars involved, I do know that from that point on, the manager took it upon himself to be a part of the solution instead of the problem—and that Mr. and Mrs. Michelson were not charged for their room.

They continued to apply these principles by expressing their appreciation to the manager for his help and consideration, and letting him know that they'd be delighted to share the story of his helpful attitude with the meeting planner.

The art of persuasion works, consistently, and often immediately.

Getting Out of a Ticket

Have you ever been pulled over by the police? It can sure be scary. Oh, no! Do I have my driver's license? Is my insurance up to date? How much is this thing going to cost? Will I have to go to traffic school?

Whatever the reason, being pulled over by the flashing blue lights can legitimately shake anyone up. There are three different ways I've noticed people handle this situation.

Some bad-mouth and insult the police officer. I'm always amazed when I see this happen. That approach will most definitely result in getting the ticket, if not landing a person in jail as well—and certainly not having that officer on your side should their help ever be needed in the future.

Others don't say a word and simply accept the ticket.

A third option is to do your very best to utilize the art of persuasion in order to avoid being given the ticket. You can guess which option I choose.

Let's say you've been pulled over for speeding. I learned this first part from a client of mine who used to be a police officer. He told me that once you've brought your car to a stop, you should turn on the inside light (if this is taking place at night) and place your hands on the steering wheel at the ten-o'clock/two-o'clock position. Do not make any sudden moves or get out of the car.

The biggest fear a police officer has is that the driver will draw a gun and shoot while the officer is approaching the vehicle. With the inside light on and you in the correct position, the officer can see that you're not a threat and you're showing the proper respect. You're making his or her job easier.

When the officer asks for your license and registration, a simple "Yes sir," or "Yes ma'am," is a great start.

The officer will probably ask if you realize you were speeding. He or she might even volunteer something like, "I clocked you at 78 in a 65 mph zone."

The best thing is not to make excuses, but instead to admit fault. "Officer, I totally believe I was going that fast, even though I didn't realize it until I saw your lights. I have no excuse. As much as I just hate to get a ticket, I am at fault."

In using this approach, you've just done the best possible job of presenting your case to the officer. You *are* guilty. You know it, and the police officer knows it. They've heard more excuses than a sixth grade teacher has about why Bobby didn't have his homework, *again*—and they won't buy it any more than Bobby's teacher did. By being honest, you have just increased the odds that the officer doesn't really *want* to give you a ticket.

If at this point you still feel you need to persuade just a bit more, you might say, "Officer, I'm definitely in the wrong. This isn't something I usually do, and I'm wondering if there's any chance of not getting a ticket, or maybe just a warning."

Then go back to the eight magic words:

If you can't do it, I'll definitely understand.

You've done everything right, showed total respect, and if the officer can now justify the situation in his or her own mind, there's a good chance you won't get a ticket. This won't work every time, but it will work *much* of the time.

It's worked for me when my foot's been just a bit heavy on the pedal or I didn't come to a complete stop at a stop sign, and it's worked for many others. I'm not recommending you make any of these mistakes. They are illegal and wrong…and because we're human, it happens. And when it does, it's still preferable not to get a ticket, as long as we learn from our mistake and do our best not to repeat it.

One time this method did not work for, the officer, a truly nice guy, told me that as much as he appreciated my attitude, he never goes back on giving someone a ticket if they're in the wrong. I was in the wrong. He gave me a ticket.

At least he was honest and polite, and I almost felt good about getting the ticket—*almost*.

Feel, Felt, Found

One of the most well-known sales techniques is the famous "feel, felt, found."

When a prospect has an objection based on a preconceived idea, and you know they're wrong, but you also know that telling them that will only offend them and keep them more firm in their belief, you make your case in a different way. That's where feel, felt, and found come into play.

It might go something like this:

"Ms. Prospect, I understand how you *feel*. Many people in your situation have *felt* the exact same way. However, in researching this further, they *found* that…" and then you finish the sentence with what's appropriate.

It's especially powerful when you include yourself in the discovery.

"I understand how you *feel*. In fact, I *felt*…" (stressing "I" instead of "many people" as you did above) "… I *felt* the exact same way. What I *found* is …" and then complete your thought in the positive.

The feel, felt, found technique also works well within the art of persuasion.

The person you are speaking with says, "That's not our policy and I don't like going against policy!" You might respond by saying, "I understand exactly how you feel. I feel the same way about our policy as an excellent foundation. What I found was that when I use policy as a foundational guide—as a *should* as opposed to a *must*—our customers are happier and the business becomes much more profitable."

You may not have changed that person's mind yet, but you are now in a position to help her without her feeling as though she's being manipulated or coerced.

Speaking of which, there is one danger when utilizing the "feel, felt, found" that needs to be considered: at this point, so many people have learned this approach that when you say those exact words *and they recognize them*, they might feel "techniqued." If that happens, rapport is broken and the effect will be the opposite of what you want.

So instead, you might want to use some alternative phrasing that follows the same general idea but doesn't adhere strictly to using those three words. For example: "That makes a lot of sense. I can certainly relate to that (I understand how you feel). I've had that same thought as you just expressed (I felt the same way). It sort of turns out that... (what I found is)."

Lincoln's Tactful Disgust Letter

Another book I highly recommend is *Lincoln on Leadership*, by Donald T. Phillips. This inspiring and very practical book displays President Lincoln's absolute mastery of the art of persuasion.

A very tactful and humble man, Lincoln would get his point across in such a way that one could not be offended, even by the president's stern criticism.

The following is a letter Lincoln wrote to General Joseph Hooker, right after Hooker was assigned to his new post. Lincoln actually handed this famous letter to the general immediately after a meeting between the two of them.

Major General Hooker: General.

I have placed you at the head of the Army of the Potomac. Of course, I have done this upon what appears to me to be sufficient reasons. And yet I think it best for you to know that there are some things in regard to which, I am not quite satisfied with you. I believe you to be a brave and skillful soldier, which, of course, I like. I also believe you do not mix politics with your profession, in which you are right. You have confidence in yourself, which is valuable, if not an indis-pensable quality. You are ambitious, which, within reasonable bounds, does good rather than harm. But I think that during Gen. Burnside's command of the Army, you have taken counsel of your ambition, and thwarted him as much as you could, in which you did a great wrong to the country, and to a most meritorious and honorable brother officer. I have heard, in such a way as to believe it, of your recently saying that both the Army and the Government needed a Dictator. Of course it was not for this, but in spite of it, that I have given you the command. Only those generals who gain successes can set up dictators. What I now ask of you is military success, and I will risk the dictatorship. The government will support you to the utmost of its ability, which is neither more nor less than it has done and will do for all commanders. I much fear that the spirit which you have aided to infuse into the Army, of criticizing their Commander, and withholding confidence from him, will now turn upon you. I shall assist you as far as I can, to put it down. Neither you, nor Napoleon, if he were alive again, could get any good out of an army, while such a spirit prevails in it.

And now, beware of rashness. Beware of rashness, but with energy, and sleepless vigilance, go forward, and give us victories.

Yours very truly,

Lincoln

I could read that letter a hundred times and not get tired of it.

Lincoln masterfully let Hooker know he was not at all happy about what he did, but first—and throughout the letter—he praised the general's many attributes.

I loved the part where he chided Hooker about expressing his belief in dictatorship. "Only those generals who gain successes can set up dictators." In other words, talk is cheap, Joe. Keep your foolish thoughts to yourself and show everyone you can actually win this thing.

What works in a letter can also work on the telephone or in person. Before criticizing, focus upon the other person's strengths. Build them up before the criticism, and afterward, too. As Lincoln so expertly did—at all times and during that letter to General Hooker—end by letting the person know you are behind him all the way and have total confidence in his abilities.

We'll talk more about the wise and diplomatic sixteenth president. As far as I'm concerned, the book *Lincoln on Leadership* is a must-read for anyone and everyone truly interested in mastering this topic.

Focus on Your Similarities as Opposed to Your Differences

We are all different, yet we are truly very much the same. When two people are trying to get what they want from each other, they usually see more differences then similarities. But when you can focus on and bring up the similarities, you are one definite step closer to mastering the art of persuasion.

Abraham Lincoln had deep personal differences with both his secretary of war, Edwin Stanton, and his secretary of state, William Seward. To show you what kind of man Lincoln was: he had hired both of them for their posts knowing the lack of appreciation and outright disrespect they both had for him. Seward even blatantly tried to undermine the president and his decisions on a number of occasions. Neither believed that Lincoln was qualified nor competent to lead the country through crisis. But each was the best qualified man for the job.

Lincoln looked for the good in both of them, the *similarities* he had with them. He found there were many, including an abiding love for and a deep commitment to their country. He began spending more time getting to know each man and having them get to know him. He was able to turn them into two of his closest and most loyal allies. That's a leader!

Remember the saying, "A mighty person is one who can control his emotions and make of an enemy a friend?" One of the many quotes attributed to Mr. Lincoln that I've always enjoyed is, "I don't like that man very much. I'm going to have to get to know him better."

When you enter into a transaction with someone whom you're attempting to win over, stretch your mind and imagination in order to focus on your similarities—and, perhaps even more importantly, make the other person aware of them as well.

This goes back to establishing rapport, and it will show you both where you actually have the same or similar goals and outcomes in mind. Once you can focus on those mutual goals, the individual challenges will begin to work themselves out naturally and automatically.

Third-party Explanations for Changing Another Person's Way of Thinking

Since no one likes to be corrected, giving someone direct criticism—unless that person's self-esteem level happens to hover around the "excellent" level—will likely deal a blow to his ego, making him more resistant to change. How do you correct someone in such a manner that he gets to save face and doesn't end up feeling defensive?

The "third-party explanation" is very effective here. Simply tell a story that puts yourself *in the role of the other person*, with you being corrected by a knowledgeable third-party.

Let's pretend your assistant has been slow in updating himself on the newest methods for using the company computer, and it's costing you time and money. You could insist that he comes in and learns what he needs to know in his spare time, or else lose his job. Will that increase his loyalty to you and improve his job performance? Probably not.

You're the boss, you could fire him. However, in every other way he is excellent, and you feel he is pretty close to indispensable. He knows you and what you like. He's personable with your clients, and they like and feel comfortable with him. So yes, you could fire him, but you'd much rather find a way to persuade him to do whatever it takes to master the newest methods for learning that computer.

Let's try the third-party explanation.

"Roger, when I first started with this company, I had a real challenge. Some of the new methods being implemented really intimidated me. My boss, Mary James—who I had a lot of respect for and who I know really appreciated my work—told me, 'You know, Bob, your value to the company will really increase if you can master this new material. After all, there're a lot of people coming right out of college who already know these things, and the best way to keep and increase your value within the company is to do whatever you have to do to keep up-to-date.'"

What happened there?

The point is made, yet you never ordered Roger to do what was necessary. You simply related, with yourself as the target, what would probably happen regarding his value to the company, depending upon the action he chose to take.

When someone you love is not doing what's needed to improve their rate of success in accomplishing their life's goals, you could say, "Hey, you need to read more books and hang around better quality people." Or you might try something more effective, the third-party explanation. "You know, a very successful man named Charlie Jones once told me 'you are the same today as you'll be in five years except for two things: the people you meet and the books you read!"

A man I admire very much once told me, "When it comes to persuading another to your point of view, the third-party explanation will go a lot further than simply telling a person what to do."

Hey, wasn't *that* a third-party explanation?

Accept the Blame and Give the Credit

You may be a leader or manager looking to accomplish team success on a long-term project. It will almost always be to your advantage to be known as a leader who is quick to take the blame for failures and quick to give away the credit for successes.

We all know of managers or supervisors whose teams slave away, yet they take the credit. Does that inspire the troops to work overtime on future projects? Does it encourage their loyalty?

No, it does not.

What if the team members get to feel the pride of being credited? How about knowing they can stretch themselves and even make mistakes without being publicly called on the carpet, because they're *safe* with you in the lead?

It's difficult to make great advancements without a few failures from which to learn, isn't it? To know the leader is with and for them all the way gives people the opportunity to grow, work harder, and produce more beneficial results for the team. If the leader takes the blame publicly, and gives them the credit publicly, their motivation and incentive is raised one-hundredfold.

As the saying goes, "It's amazing what you can accomplish if you don't care who gets the credit." As the leader, which do you want more, the victory or the credit? The paradox is, when you do this consistently, you'll end up getting even more credit than you would have otherwise.

This was another area in which Abraham Lincoln excelled. According to Donald T. Phillips in *Lincoln on Leadership*, during the president's last public address before his assassination, he exclaimed to the crowd, "No part of the honor, for plan or execution, is mine. To General Grant, his skillful officers, and brave men, all belongs."

Everyone knows how hard and skillfully Lincoln worked during the war. People will know about your efforts as well. The less you congratulate yourself, the more your reputation will continue to *do it for you* in the eyes of both your team and the public.

Being Snubbed or Disrespected

When someone you'll be seeing again snubs you or acts disrespectful, you may feel it's something you just cannot or should not ignore. Still, a personal confrontation may not achieve the desired results. When this is the case, don't call her on it right then and there. Instead, keep your attitude positive and from then on stay polite while simply showing "subtle signs" of displeasure.

Let's take the case of a waitress at a brand new restaurant I'd been patronizing since they opened. I had always treated her with respect, as I try to do with everyone, and had always left generous tips. But her service and attitude began to change in a negative way, which affected my dining experience. From then on, I showed the same level of respect and politeness, but was just a little bit less outgoing and responsive, and tipped her significantly less.

She came around really quickly.

I don't believe it was just the lessening of tip, although I'm certain that got her attention. People sense when you're not quite behaving the same way toward them, especially when you are normally friendly and complimentary. If you remain polite, but forgo the other qualities you usually display, they'll understand that something is wrong and will usually correct it all by themselves.

If they come right out and ask, "Is anything wrong?" then you have the opportunity—in a very polite way—to explain. (And by the way, this is a perfect opportunity to use the *I message* we discussed earlier.)

You may be asking, "If somebody does something that bothers you, why not just let them know right then and there, rather than playing games?"

The answer is, depending upon the situation, letting them know right then and there may not be the most effective course of action. There are times when it is, and if that's the case, of course take care of it right away by being respectfully direct. However, when you suspect that doing so will be not as productive, or you don't feel the person will be able to handle it without being defensive, then you can employ this more subtle, indirect approach. It will work *much* more often than not.

Persuade by Playing One Source Off the Other

Remember when, as a kid, you'd play one parent off the other when negotiating for a certain result? You'd say, "Mom, can I go over to Joey's?" Your mom would tell you to ask your dad. So you'd go to you dad—but instead of *asking* him, "Can I go over to Joey's?" if you were really resourceful, you'd say, "Dad, I told Mom I'm going to Joey's, and she just wants me to get your okay first."

Positions things a little bit differently, doesn't it?

Guess what? You can use that approach as a grownup as well!

When I was a television news anchor, I was known for having a knack for being able to get on-air comments from newsmakers who usually didn't want to comment at all. And I was certainly *not* a journalist—I was simply a good *reader* of news. There's a big difference.

On the other hand, the reporter I was teamed with, named Jackie, was an excellent journalist with a deep understanding of the issues and an ability to put together a story that could truly educate and involve people. The running joke between us was that Jackie could never figure out how someone like me, with such an amazing lack of understanding of journalism, could get practically anyone to talk to him.

How? I simply used the technique of playing one source off the other.

Here's an example: Mayor Hyman would generally be on one side of an issue and Commissioner Balbontin on the other. Each would refuse to be interviewed by the media. I would get on the phone and first call Mayor Hyman. With a sound of indignation in my voice I would say, "Mr. Mayor, this issue is being heard by a lot of people, and I will absolutely *not* give the commissioner air time without you having a chance to state your position on the matter. Absolutely not!" He would thank me and agree to go on the air.

I could then tell the commissioner that the mayor had the opportunity to air his views, and I would "absolutely *not* allow that without giving you, Mr. Commissioner, the opportunity to do the same. It's only fair."

You can do the same thing in practically any area of persuasion.

"Ms. Sales Prospect, we are rolling out our product in your area beginning next month, and I absolutely refuse to present it to your competition without at least giving you the opportunity to learn about it as well."

Be sure and choose the right situation to use this. It won't work unless the setting is right, with two or more people who can be equally affected.

In the right circumstances it works like a charm.

Winning with Intimidation (Only as a Last Resort, of Course)

Every so often a situation arises where the only way you can get what you want is by intimidating the right person at the right time. This is not something I love doing, but if there's no other choice and time is of the essence, you do what you have to do.

I was heading out to the local airport to get a quick comment on camera with then Governor Bob Graham. Surprisingly enough, my camera person and I were the only news media there, but I guess the others figured they'd do their interviews at the big meeting he'd be addressing later that evening. With camera in hand, we went to greet his private plane.

Unfortunately, we couldn't find out where it was landing. Obviously, this information was not for public or media knowledge. We saw a car at an intersection, and we asked the people in the car if they knew where the governor's plane would be landing. They assured us they had no idea, but something told me they weren't being 100 percent truthful.

We kept our eye on their car and trailed them to the landing sight. As we pulled up, the head person—the very same one who assured us they had no idea what was happening—admitted that, "Yes, this is the governor's plane, but he wasn't planning on any interviews until tonight."

Like many people, I hate being lied to—so there was no way I was *not* going to get that interview, and get it right now.

Still attempting to be polite, I said, "Well, we'd appreciate a short sound bite, if you'd be so kind as to arrange it." He patronizingly replied that he'd just said that wasn't in the plans, but we were welcomed to get one tonight. Knowing that he wasn't going to be interested in the fact that now I wanted an exclusive, especially since I had hustled out to the airport when none of the others had, I didn't bother mentioning it. I said, "Well, let's give the governor an opportunity to tell his constituents how happy he is to be in this fine city, and then I'll ask him one quick question about his speech tonight." His response, with a touch of superiority in his voice, was, "Well, that will be up to the governor, won't it?"

It was now time to win *with* intimidation, because that was the only option I could see working. I looked toward my camera person and said, "Ellen, roll the camera starting right now. We'll get a nice shot of the plane landing, and the governor coming out and walking right past us into his car, refusing to address the citizens of this area. And we'll have the camera and microphone right there, so that the viewers can form their own opinions of his silence."

That was a ludicrous, meaningless threat if there ever was one. I also knew it would be easier for them to get him in front of the camera for a few words than explain to him later why they allowed a jerky reporter like myself to cause any kind of trouble. There was no reason for him not to do a quick interview. His aide was just displaying his power. (Ego, remember?) The man met his boss at the plane and obviously told him the right thing, because the governor walked toward us, all smiles. He was quite gracious.

It was an easy interview, we got our story, he looked good, and we all lived happily ever after.

Slight intimidation is sometimes necessary. However, I vastly prefer to use that only as a last resort. I would rather have won over that aide with kindness, and then have been in a position to have him on my side later on if needed.

Fortunately, it never was—needed, I mean. But how can you ever know for sure? Plus, it's just nice to be able to be nice.

Making the Best out of an Uncomfortable Situation

After that on-the-tarmac interview just described, the governor chatted with us and asked for our cards—mine and Ellen's. I'm not sure why, possibly to give us a feeling of importance. After all, it was people like us—the press—that he really wanted on his side.

No wonder he's a successful politician. He later became a U.S. senator and remains popular to this day.

He made the best out of an uncomfortable situation for both himself and his aide. For all the governor knew or was told about the situation, I was a reporter out to get him. I wasn't, but that's probably what his aide told him.

The governor, though, was out to do the right thing: turn a potential enemy into a friend. That's someone who understands the art of persuasion.

Be Consistent in Your Actions

Consistency of action is an important part of every powerful persuader's repertoire. After all, we live in a very inconsistent world, filled with very inconsistent people. We all know people who run hot and cold. They are *this* way one day and *that* way the next. It makes life that much more difficult for everyone around them.

Maybe I'm simply describing their personality. One minute he is the nicest person in the world, the next, a virtual monster. She says one thing one minute, and the next moment seems to have totally changed her mind. These types are annoying at best, and nearly impossible to relate to work with (or work *for*) at worst. You never know where you stand with these people.

On the other hand, what about the rocks of the world—those rare, consistently consistent people who have been, are, and will always be the same? Not in a boring way; just a consistent way. There is a comfort in being around those people, isn't there?

Negotiating authority Roger Dawson suggests that this was exactly what made Ronald Reagan so popular and successful as a politician. He was consistent. You could count on him. People knew where he would stand on any issue that came up. Regardless of whether they agreed with his view or not, people felt secure in their knowledge of him as a leader. What he stood for yesterday was what he stood for today and what he would stand for tomorrow.

I was watching a news report showing speeches the president made when he was running for governor of California some twenty years earlier. His words were nearly exactly the same then as they were during his campaign for the presidency. People laughed at that, as though he had been "found out." But that's exactly what made him so successful! People of any political belief always knew where Mr. Reagan stood.

It's the same as the young child who can have only one piece of chocolate for dessert or can watch only thirty minutes of television per evening. He might not agree with your decision, but he feels very secure in the fact that he knows his limits with you. He's secure with your sense of consistency in decision-making.

It's a good way to earn people's trust as a president; it's a good way to make a child feel secured and cared for. And it's a good way to make *everyone* around you feel good, too.

Bring Up Their Side of the Issue First—and Only Then, Yours

When negotiating or involved in a disagreement, always present the other person's case first.

This is a tactic Abraham Lincoln applied quite often as an attorney. As I mentioned earlier, Lincoln would often begin arguing his case by highlighting the strong points of the *other* side's case. If a person didn't know better, they would think he was representing the opposition! He covered facts he knew would be brought up by the opposition anyway, but in bringing them up first, he had an opportunity to show his sense of fair play.

This softened the natural defense mechanism of the judge and jurors who were inevitably expecting to hear a one-sided monologue. What Lincoln did, in essence, is communicate, "Hey, I'm looking at this case strictly from merit as a fair and open-minded person. Just seeking the truth—as *you* are."

He firmly established his honesty, integrity, and sense of fair play and justice. A pretty winning place to start for an attorney, don't you think? Of course, he would then present a much stronger case for his side, which, because of the jury's positive feelings toward him, was even more persuasive and effective.

When you are in a situation with another person where there is a definite difference of opinion, you can apply this with great success. Present some of the facts from their side first to essentially say, "Hey, clearly there are two sides to our discussion. We're both reasonable, nice people who have points we believe in."

That's mastering the art of persuasion.

8

What Sets You Apart from the Rest

Remain Humble After Your Victory

Whether it's only a game of Monopoly® played with friends or a big sale in which you've won out over your competition, *never* gloat or act cocky. Always be humble.

If you aren't, the other players will go out of their way to make sure you don't win next time, even if *they* have to lose just to keep you from winning. That's simply human nature.

Positive Persuasion via the Platinum Rule

Prolific authors Jim Cathcart and Dr. Tony Allesandra often speak on the topic of what *relationship selling*, and are especially well known for what they call the Platinum Rule.

The age-old Golden Rule is, "Do unto others as you'd have them do unto you." Isn't that a wonderful philosophy to have? According to Jim and Tony, the Platinum Rule goes one giant step further: "Do unto others as *they'd like* to be done unto."

They explain that distinct personality types and styles have different ways they like to be treated or dealt with in various situations. This of course relates not only to professional sales but to all facets of persuasion in your life and work.

Some people want the bottom line right away. Others want to know all the details, facts, and figures. Certain people want to take time to get to know each other and establish a friendship. Others want to be continually assured that they're making the right decision. Some people want to be worked with and negotiated with *like this*, and other people want to be worked with and negotiated with *like that*.

If you want to increase your odds of success in any and all personal transactions, learn how other people want to be treated—and then treat them that way.

Request Rather than Order

If you really want to distinguish yourself from the masses, try making requests instead of issuing orders. A person who is used to being *ordered* to perform, such as a waitperson, staff member, or hotel employee, will go absolutely out of his way to serve you if you *request* his actions.

Instead of saying to the waiter, "Bring us some more water," or, "We need water," you might say, "When you get a chance, would you please bring us some more water?" Some might think this would only delay getting the water.

Actually, the opposite is true. Because you've made that person feel respected, you'll be the *first* person he'll want to make happy.

Rather than making it an order, make it a request. Instead of, "Joe, make seven copies of these," how about, "Joe, would you run seven copies of these for me, please?"

Phrase your "order" in the form of a request, and you'll be persuading effectively both in the short- and long-term.

Be a "Yes Person"

I don't mean the stereotypical *yes man* who is always sucking up to the boss. Rather, I'm talking about being the person who, when approached by someone with a new idea, looks for the good in it, for the possibilities, rather than what's wrong or what won't work.

Of course, I'm not suggesting you should say something you don't believe, or lie, or take action on every idea that comes up. Not at all. Each idea and action must be judged on its own merit. I'm saying simply to be encouraging, whether it's a request from a vendor or a friend looking for encouragement regarding a new idea.

Most people look at the negative. When approached with an idea, they respond with, "That'll never work." How about a request from a vendor to look at a new product or service? They typically say things like, "It's not our policy... It's never been done before..." or, "I don't think we can do that."

While the approaches we're reviewing in this pages are designed to help to overcome such attitudes in others, we also need to be aware of them in ourselves. Even if you do in fact feel that nothing can be done, be supportive. Instead of immediately discouraging the other person, give whatever positive response you can.

You may not agree with a vendor's idea and you may not see the possibilities your friend envisions, but you can certainly root for them all the way. Let them know you're pulling for them. Offer whatever best wishes and emotional support you can give.

This results in others seeing you as a source of emotional support, and one for whom they have true appreciation.

The Letter That's Never Sent

Have you ever been very angry—furious, perhaps enraged—at someone who mistreated you? Here's a suggestion: write a scathing, insulting letter. Let it all hang out. Don't hold back. Put it in an envelope, address that envelope, and even put a stamp on it if you like.

Then, before mailing that letter, tear it up into a thousand pieces.

Your anger will have subsided dramatically, and no one will ever know.

Author and speaker Zig Ziglar gave that wise piece of advice to a woman who approached him after a program to tell him of a personal situation she had gone through which really aroused her resentment. I was a young speaker who had opened for Zig that day, and I was standing right there as that great man took time to listen patiently and then carefully counsel this person (immediately after having just performed one of his high-energy presentations).

Sometimes it is correct to send a letter expressing resentment of a situation. In such cases, it's far better to do so *after* first waiting a few days before writing it, and even then, to express your feelings as diplomatically as you can.

In this case, though, Zig suggested a different strategy, and it was the perfect piece of advice.

This was another of Abe Lincoln's techniques, too. Sometimes he needed to express his angry feelings just to get it all off his chest, so he'd write a letter with every scathing remark and insult he could think of, and then tear it up or file it away forever.

How to know which approach is appropriate? You can judge the situation this way: if no one would benefit from that letter being sent, and people might be unnecessarily hurt, then you can assume the letter would not add positively to the situation. In that case, the best thing you can do is to never send it.

But do write it! Writing that letter is wonderful therapy. You'll get your negative feelings off your chest and be very glad you did.

Who wants to carry anger like that around? Why would anyone want to?

Edify, Edify, Edify

As we said earlier, to *edify* means to *build*. When you edify a person to someone else, you build them up in that other person's mind. When you edify him to himself, you build him in his own mind. The more you do that, the better he'll feel about himself and the better he'll feel about you, too.

Edifying someone to a third party plays on the old saying, "If you can't say something nice, don't say anything at all." And the truth is, you can *always* say something nice about someone, and you can always find a reason to do so.

Even the most miserable people out there have something about them that we can discover and edify to someone else. This accomplishes two things: first, it will probably get back to that person you are edifying, which can only have positive results. And second, you'll establish yourself in the mind of *the person you're speaking to* as someone who only has nice things to say about other people.

People enjoy people who are like that, and certainly much more so than those who speak negatively of others. And even if *they* are the kind who speak negatively about others, they'll still respect you for your edification of others.

My Dad is a tremendous example of a man who only speaks positively and with edification of others. From his wife (my Mom) to his kids, his friends, and even people who, to most others, warrant only unkind words, Dad will always find something nice to say—and sometimes it can involve a search and a stretch to do so!

Husbands and wives often talk about how the love and respect has gone out of their marriage. In such situations, I often notice how they don't seem to have the habit of edifying each other, either to themselves or to other people. My folks are *always* edifying or bragging on each other, and they have for as long as I can remember.

Do you suppose there is a correlation between to the success of a marriage—or a friendship, or business relationship—and how those involved talk about each other behind their backs, as well as right in front of them?

See if you notice how this works in your own relationships and the relationships of those around you.

My Favorite Dad Story

With the foregoing in mind, I have to relate an incident that embodies the essence of edification while displaying incredible tact and diplomacy.

When I was about ten or eleven years old, we were having a brand new carpet installed in our home. During the day, we all stayed in one room while the crew boss and his two assistants were laying down the carpet in the rest of the house. The boss was a decent person, but one of those rough around the edges, beer-guzzling, hard-living guys who would probably belong to Ralph Kramden's Raccoon Lodge from *The Honeymooners*. (Nothing wrong with that, of course: just painting a picture for you.)

At lunchtime, my folks bought pizza for us and the crew. Dad went upstairs to bring the pizza to the carpet-layers and talk with the crew boss about how things were coming along. Since Dad is a great guy and can relate to practically anybody, the boss naturally wanted to ingratiate himself, and the male bonding process was soon underway, as I sat around the corner listening to their conversation.

The boss began by saying, "Hey, this is some expensive job. Boy-oh-boy, those women will really spend your money for you, won't they?"

Dad responded by saying, "Well, I'll tell you, when they were right there with you before you *had* any money, it's a pleasure to do anything for them you possibly can, isn't it?"

That's not exactly the answer this guy expected. He was looking for this to be a conversation between two guys who could talk negatively about their wives. To him, that was the natural thing for men to do. So he tried again:

"But, gee, they'll really play off that and want to spend all they can, won't they?"

Dad replied exactly as I knew he would: "Hey, when they're the reason for your success, you really want to know you're doing things they enjoy. There's no greater pleasure."

Strike two. The crew boss tried one more time. "And, uh…they'll take that as far as they can, huh?"

Dad responded: "It's just so gratifying to know you've got a wife who's your best friend, and you'd do anything within your power to make her happy."

At this point, I was working hard to keep from laughing, because I knew the guy wanted Dad to at least give in a little bit and say, "Yeah, yeah, I guess that's true." But I knew that wouldn't happen. Not in a million years.

Finally, the boss gave up. Maybe he learned something in that transaction about respecting one's spouse. Maybe not. It taught a young boy a lot, though, about the power of respect and edification.

My Mom and Dad would do anything for each other. After learning about that conversation, would you have any doubt?

You can use this principle not only to succeed in your married life but also in dealing with people in general. If people know you are edifying them, that will lead to long-term relationship success.

Giving Yourself the Advantage Through Delayed Gratification

Someone wrongs you. It happens, doesn't it? It certainly does to me. Respond or react? Look to get even, or keep your head?

Before reacting negatively toward the person or their actions, pause and ask yourself, "Will my reaction strengthen or hurt my relationship or position with this person?"

It might feel good in the short term to strike back, but, in the long run, will it most likely be productive or counterproductive?

The answer is obvious, isn't it?

You *always* have a choice between instant gratification and delayed gratification. Those who consistently come out ahead are the ones who opt for the delayed variety.

There's No Winning an Argument

It was in Dale Carnegie's book, *How to Win Friends and Influence People*, that I first learned the principle that there really is no way to win an argument. As Mr. Carnegie so famously said, "A man convinced against his will is of the same opinion still." Not to mention the bad will that will probably result with that person.

Abe Lincoln agreed. In *Lincoln on, Leadership*, Donald T. Phillips relates how the president reprimanded Captain

James M. Cutts for continually arguing with and verbally abusing another officer. Lincoln pointed out that no person resolved to make the most of himself can spare time for personal conflict. The most famous part of his reprimand was the following:

> Better to give your path to a dog, than be bitten by him in contesting for the right. Even killing the dog would not cure the bite.

When in the persuasion process, I recommend you do your best never to argue.

We've been reviewing ideas throughout this book on how to effectively persuade people and get what you want *without* letting ourselves be drawn into an argument, but every so often, despite our best intentions, we feel ourselves slipping in that argumentative direction.

When this happens, remember the lessons from Dale Carnegie and Abraham Lincoln on the uselessness of arguing. They will serve you, perhaps better than any other single skill, in your quest to master the art of persuasion.

Lose the Battle, Win the War

Sometimes it's okay to lose a small battle in order to win the bigger overall victory. When negotiating or attempting to win your point, don't be afraid to make some minor concessions here and there to get what you're *really* after. You've got to be able to see the big picture.

We discussed earlier that people who have only a certain amount of power don't like to have that power undermined. Even if you succeed in convincing them that you're right (and that's a big *if*), their ego will likely prevent you from persuading them to change their thought or action.

Instead, why not let them save face by winning a couple of unimportant points that really don't matter much to you? This will allow them to feel as though they didn't get beaten into the ground, and that they won, as well. Which, if they come away feeling good about themselves, they *did*.

Sometimes you may even have to invent those small points for them to win. When you do, take care to let the other person feel that point was *their* brainchild, *their* victory. With a little imagination it's easy to do, and the dividends will be well worth it.

Complaints with Humility Get Better Responses

When writing a letter of complaint or leaving a complaint on voice mail, state the facts with humility. If possible, begin your communication with praise. Mention that you certainly don't know nearly as much about that person's position or business as do they. Then, when you point out an observation that is right on the mark—even if it's not positive—your credibility with that person increases even more.

After visiting several different stores of a particular franchise operation and receiving absolutely terrible service at each and every one, I decided to call the company headquarters and voice my displeasure to the CEO himself. He wasn't in, but I did reach his voice mail and decided to simply leave a message.

Since this event took place several years ago, and it didn't occur to me that there might be a need to remember my words verbatim for reproducing in a book, I can only give you a paraphrase of my message. I know I can get close to the original words, though, because I would use this same method any time I was in a similar situation. The message went something like this:

> Hi Mr. Smith, this is Bob Burg calling from Jupiter, Florida. If you'd *like* to call me after hearing this message you're welcome to, but it certainly isn't necessary. I'm a very loyal and usually quite satisfied customer who has enjoyed using and referring your products for years. I thought you might be interested in a few incidents at your Florida stores.
>
> Unfortunately—and very unlike my usual experience with your company's excellent customer service people—I was put in a very challenging situation that didn't work to the advantage of your store, myself, or the other customers. Had this event happened once, even twice, I'd have shrugged it off, knowing your company's dedication to your customers. After three separate occurrences—although I don't pretend to know your business—quite frankly, I thought you might want to know.
>
> If you'd like to speak with me further, again, my name is Bob Burg and I'm at 561-555-5555. Thank you for your time. Make it a great day.

Do you think I received a response from this huge corporation?

I sure did. Not from the CEO himself, but from his right-hand man. We spoke on the phone, and not only was he very apologetic, he was very grateful that I called and made him aware of the situation.

People in that position place a lot more importance on a complaint made by someone who acts humbly, logically, and civilly. Troubleshooters have to deal with ranters, ravers, and screamers all day long. They are a dime a dozen... or maybe more like a penny.

By positioning yourself politely apart from the negative crowd, you increase your chances dramatically of obtaining the satisfaction you desire.

Treat Everyone the Exact Same Way— with R-E-S-P-E-C-T

The Platinum Rule, as mentioned a bit earlier, says that we should treat every individual in the way *they* want to be treated. In a larger sense, though, it's best to strive to treat *every* person—in every job, position, or station in life—the same way and with the same respect as you would, say, a millionaire CEO of a Fortune 500 company.

Not only is it the right thing to do (and, it is!), but you never know when you're going to need that person for something important. That's one reason why it's so important to learn these habits.

Yes, it happens by way of habit: when the action is so ingrained that you do it without thinking.

Do you show respect to the man or woman at the toll gate? How about the waitperson? The person at the cash register? The custodian?

Making this show of respect a habit leads to both short- and long-term success with others.

A Good Test

When you feel good about yourself, knowing you're acting out of fairness and kindness, focusing on providing value to the lives of others, it shows up in your general demeanor and goes a long way toward both your personal and professional success.

As a personal test to make sure you're staying on the right track, ask yourself, "Is what I'm doing serving the other person, as well as myself?"

Yes, it's as simple as that.

Match and Mirror

Earlier we looked at Neuro-Linguistic Programming, or NLP, a technology that is very effective in helping to establish rapport. One way of using NLP to create rapport is to physically match or mirror the other person.

How does one do this? Here's an example: as the person you're with begins to rest her hand on her chin—or cross her legs, or fold her arms—wait for a moment, and then slowly do the same.

Of course, you don't want to be obvious. If the person senses you are doing this intentionally, it will tend to come across as manipulative, and if that happens, you'll lose any rapport you have built thus far.

Actually, the chances are very good that you *already* do this, at least in some situations. Matching and mirroring are totally natural processes when two people are already in rapport. You're simply helping the process, so the other person feels comfortable with you sooner rather than later.

Even matching another person's breathing can do wonders. With a little practice, it's a snap. According to NLP authority Susan Stageman of Dallas, Texas, when done correctly, matching breathing brings two people totally in sync.

Can you see how this would help greatly in the persuasion process?

You can also match the volume of the person's voice. If she's talking softly, just do the same thing. You can also increase your tempo to match her speed, or speak a little more slowly if that's what she is doing.

In establishing rapport over the telephone, voice matching can be very effective.

Again, none of this is meant to manipulate and persuade someone to do something they wouldn't normally do. It is simply a method to enhance the speed and power with which you can build a natural rapport.

Obvious...but Utilized?

Treat a person with kindness and respect, and they'll go out of their way for you a lot quicker and a lot more strongly than if you yell, insult, or threaten them.

Totally obvious, right? Then why do we see so many people yelling, insulting, and threatening people?

This is something worth thinking about the next time you feel yourself about to react to someone else's actions (or inactions). How much better could you make your chances of winning through the art of persuasion by simply responding with kindness, compassion, and respect?

Make Sure Your Compliments Are Related to the Intended Person

Tell the manager you hope she'll let the waitperson know that her service was fantastic. Tell the waitperson that the food was wonderful, and to please pass that compliment on to the chef.

You want to make sure your compliments about another person get heard *by* that person. You also want them to know from whom the compliment originated.

Why?

Because, not only will they feel good about it—a reward from you for their excellent service—but they'll also feel good *about you* and be even more anxious to please you the next time you come in.

Does this really work? Absolutely! I've had chefs come out of the kitchen and walk over to my table to personally thank me for my kind words.

And by the way, this isn't only about restaurant service. It works in virtually any area in which you desire to win with people.

A Restaurant Tip that Gets Results

Speaking of restaurants, when sending food back to be recooked or cooked differently, or because of any other challenge, address the waitperson beginning with these words: "Please, tell the chef the dinner is absolutely excellent. There's just one thing, if I could have…" and finish the request with what you want.

Remember to make sure the waitperson intends to share the praise. Watch how nicely your meal comes out this time.

Don't be surprised if the chef comes out to personally make sure all is as it should be.

Just a Thought

Each and every year, millions of ¼-inch drill bits are sold, yet nobody buying any one of these ¼-inch drill bits actually wants a ¼-inch drill bit.

Then why do they buy them? Because they want a ¼-inch *hole*.

What's my point, and what does this have to do with the art of persuasion? People do things, not for the thing itself, but for the benefit that doing the thing brings them.

What makes this challenging is those reasons are not always obvious. But without our knowing what they are, the chances of their taking the action we desire them to take are considerably lowered.

The key is to find out by asking the right questions. In sales, not everyone has the same buying motivation. Some base their decision on price, others on quality, and still others on style or convenience. Your job is to find out in order to help them get the "¼-inch hole" they want.

Outside of sales, not everyone reacts or responds to a situation for the same reasons we might. When attempting to persuade, you have to know what their ¼-inch hole is. Once you do that, you're most of the way there.

A Quick Telephone Tip

For sure-fire, long-term success, especially if the relationship you are establishing is one you are cultivating is via phone, here's a simple tip that will always work for you.

It will never come back to haunt you, either. I learned this from telephone sales authority David Allan Yoho. Are you ready?

Hang up last.

Isn't it a lousy feeling when just a nanosecond after saying good-bye to someone, you hear the loud, impersonal *click* of the telephone being plunked down on its holder? And even if *you* don't find it annoying, many people do. More than just annoying, in fact. It gives most people the feeling that, "Hey, that person really wanted to get off the phone with me. I wonder why… Am I just another sale or number to them?"

To ensure that this doesn't happen, make sure you give the other person time to hang up the phone first. If you feel that person, for whatever reason, is waiting for you to hang up first, just wait a few seconds, and then gently, carefully, hang up the phone.

This takes practice to become a habit. I always let new office staff know that this is very important to me, and I found that I had to remind them to make it a habit.

If I was walking past someone's desk and heard him hang up quickly after saying good-bye, I questioned him about it. A few times the employee would say, "Oh, I was just talking to a friend, someone I know really well."

"Doesn't matter," I replied. "What we do as a bad habit in one context, we'll tend to do all the time."

To make sure we get the full advantage of this neat tip, we have to completely replace that old habit with this new and more positive habit.

Good Morning!

It never hurts to smile and greet people cheerfully.

People are never exactly sure how your attitude will be when you're approaching them. Most people deal with many unhappy, even mean and nasty people. That's what they've learned to expect. When you smile and say, "Good morning," you've set the tone for everybody to win.

But please, don't ever say, "How ya doing?" Actually, most people don't even pronounce the "g" at the end, so it's more like, "How ya doin?" When a person says, "How ya doin'?" doesn't it sound a bit like they are actually saying, "I don't really care *how ya doin'…?*"

Few things come across as less sincere than when someone says "How ya doin'?" as they continue to walk right past you without waiting for an answer. And they're *not* waiting for an answer, because in actuality, it's a non-greeting.

In *your* greeting, always be sincere. If you say, "How ya doin?" are you really asking them to stop what they're doing and tell you how things are going for them right now in their lives? Is that a conversation you're truly inviting? If not, then don't. Find a greeting that embodies something that you truly mean.

For example, "Good morning!"

Recently I crossed paths with a person, and as our eyes met, it was obvious he wasn't very happy. One option would have been to just ignore him completely, but would I really have been making any contribution to the world that way? I flashed a big grin and said, "Good morning!" And I meant it.

I wish you could have seen his face brighten as he smiled and greeted me in return.

Maybe he greeted someone the same way a bit after that, and maybe that person did the same to someone else. If you figure those people will all have a much healthier attitude as they encounter other people during the day, think how many lives were potentially affected positively with that one brief greeting. It made us both feel better about ourselves at the same time. There wasn't any cost, but there sure was a reward.

Actually, two rewards: one was the good feeling we both got from giving the greeting, and the other was having the change to practice *internalizing* greeting someone the right way.

This habit comes in handy. *Very* handy.

Another Way of Asking

One way to get someone on your side really quickly is to apologize.

Sound strange?

"*I'm sorry* to bother you, could you please…" and then complete your request. Asking in that way will more often than not elicit a quick and helpful response. This is true whether you're asking someone on the street for directions or asking a government bureaucrat a question about the form you need to fill out.

You're making the person feel needed and acknowledging to him that you know he is important enough to have his time constraints considered. You're being humble and courteous.

This simple approach to reaching out to another person for assistance has helped me win without intimidation many times through the years.

Beginning a Telephone Sale

When calling someone on the phone, here's a good way to begin the conversation and clear the moment. You may need their time to listen to your sales presentation, or maybe you need a special exemption from your kid's principal. Doesn't matter what the situation is, it still works.

Simply say something like, "Ms. Conrad, this is Bob Burg, do you have a quick minute, or did I call at a really awful time?"

There are people from the old school of sales who'll say, "Burg, why would you give this person an opportunity to get rid of you?"

That's not what I'm doing.

If she answers, "Actually, yes, I'm in the middle of a conference and I'm surrounded by four clients with a deadline for completion on another project in thirty minutes," then you can pretty safely assume you wouldn't have had her full attention anyway. In fact, you would only have caused her to resent you, which would make obtaining your end goal a whole lot more difficult.

What the other usually says will be either, "Well, I've got a few minutes, how may I help you?" or, "No, this is fine."

By showing him you respect his time, you are honoring him and making him feel good about himself. And of course, that will more quickly establish rapport, which leads to the outcome you desire.

Confessing Ignorance

Can you and I put our egos aside in order to get what we want? If not, let's work on it. It's a key to mastering the art of persuasion.

You can always easily confess your ignorance in the area that the person with whom you're dealing is skilled. Only if it's true of course, but usually you're willing to pay someone a fee to perform a particular job or service because they specialize in that particular area (and you don't).

In my case, it's easy to admit ignorance in many areas and be totally truthful about it. As I mentioned earlier, it's easy for me to tell the mechanic, "Sue, I am the most ignorant person in the world when it comes to cars."

You might be thinking: Burg, didn't you just set yourself up to be taken advantage of? No, I don't think so. I have just used the method we discussed earlier, of putting my fate in this person's hands in a way that makes her feel important. It makes her feel good about herself—and if anything, that's more likely to lead her to do a *better* job, not a sloppier one.

What this approach has done is to pave the way for her to want to take good care of me. People are like that. We all like to use our skills for the benefit of others—especially when those others seek our help with politeness and respect.

I've confessed ignorance in countless situations, and I tend to get treated better and more fairly than most other people—certainly better than those who take the opposite approach!

A Key Thought

Please keep this thought in mind continually. In essence, it's what this book is all about and why it's so very possible to consistently find yourself obtaining what you desire when dealing with others. Here's the thought:

Make people feel good about themselves!

This is so important, I want to repeat it.

Make people feel good about themselves!

Keep that continually at top of mind, and your life will become a whole lot easier.

Admit Mistakes

For some reason, there are people who have a real challenge doing this one, yet it's really so simple and effective, and it actually causes people to admire you even more. It's such a simple thing, and it's one we just discussed a few pages back. Do you know what it is?

Apologize.

Apologize when you are wrong. Sometimes even if you aren't.

Umh! I apologize. I was wrong.

Look at your own life and work. Isn't the level of respect you have for people who will admit their mistakes and apologize much higher than for the people who refuse to do this?

We humans seem to have a challenge with apologizing—with friends, family, coworkers, and practically everyone else. If we can get past that and simply admit when we're wrong, we'll have one more effective power tool we can plug in and use for increasing our effectiveness with others.

In his powerful book, *Dynamic People Skills*, Dexter Yager writes, "One thing I do when potential conflicts arise with people is to apologize. Most people are afraid to apologize for anything at all. That's because they don't understand the power of it."

He then adds, "I'll apologize at the drop of a hat. I'll apologize for things that are my fault and things that are not my fault. I've found out that apologies are magical. They take the pressure off the situation, off the other person and put it on me. That stops conflict immediately."

What I appreciate most about Dexter's message is the fact that when we can do this—apologize when we are wrong *and especially when we aren't*—it shows a tremendous amount of self-confidence and self-esteem. Your gesture will ultimately be appreciated by the other person, and you will have gained a great deal of respect at the same time.

Focus on the Solution, Not the Problem

Those of us who practice the art of persuasion realize that, day after day, we must persuade those who are lazy, stubborn, arrogant, unimaginative, or whatever else, to find ways to do things they ordinarily would not do. Just think about how often you hear someone respond to your request with, "We don't do it that way here," or, "It's not our policy," or, "Sorry, it can't be done." Or the always magical, "I tried it once and it doesn't work."

My good friend Thomas Hudson has some excellent advice for this situation. He calls it "living in the solution, not the problem."

You do that anyway, don't you? Sure you do. Your challenge, then, is to get the *other* person to do that: to help that person out of the problem mode and into the solution mode. This means tactfully letting that person know you are both going into that mode, and together you'll come up with a solution. As much as you possibly can, let the other person feel that the solution was theirs. As long as you do this with an attitude of kindness and helpfulness, it will work.

Becoming solution-oriented applies in matters of the heart as well as business. Dexter Yager points out that "when a problem develops in a relationship, your goal is to solve the problem, not win the war." This relates beautifully to all aspects of persuasion, doesn't it?

Mr. Yager suggests that we need to put ego (the normal human desire to be right) aside and not let that desire control us. He says that if we *do* let desire take over, we confuse the issue and contaminate the situation until no one can distinguish the true problem, let alone its solution.

He continues, "Most people in a conflict situation haven't taken time to figure out what they want themselves, much less what the other person wants."

The way to ensure this doesn't happen is to start with the solution in mind.

9

Nuggets of Wisdom
Learned Along the Way

If You Could Prove to Yourself That...

The smallest change in phraseology can make a big difference in how your ideas come across to another person.

Has anyone ever said to you, perhaps while simply attempting to prove a point or wanting you to buy something from them, "If I can convince you that (such and such) will save you money..." or, "If I can prove to you that..." And didn't you sort of say to yourself, "This guy isn't going to convince me of anything!" I know I have. It's human nature to resist when challenged, and the phrases "If I can convince you" or "If I can prove to you that" are certainly challenge.

Here's a more effective way to open someone to your "proof," and it's another gem I first learned from Zig Ziglar: instead of saying, "If I can convince you that…" say, "If you could *convince yourself* that…" Then continue with the benefit you want them to understand, such as "… that this will save you money in the long run." Or, "If you could *prove to yourself* that the right way is to…"

Now you've allowed that person to take control and convince herself or prove something to herself. Who is she going to resist—herself and her own ideas? No way!

Practice this enough so that when the situation arises, the correct way of phrasing your point will come out naturally. After all, if you could convince yourself that this idea would help you to more effectively persuade, wouldn't you want to perfect it?

I Might Be Wrong about This…

This is another of those lead-in phrases that makes a person more receptive to your request or challenge. It's very simple and goes like this:

"Mr. Thomas, I might be wrong about this—*it certainly wouldn't be the first time*. I'm wondering, though…" and then fill in the rest with your particular challenge or request.

Do you need to tell a manager about an error on your bill?

"I might be wrong about this. I'm wondering though, wasn't this charge right here only $17 instead of $117?"

That's much more effective than telling others they are wrong and must fix it, and is much more likely to get you the results you desire.

Win without Intimidation, Just by Listening

There are times when absolutely the best thing we can do in order to prove our point is to listen—really listen—to the *other* person. Just listen until they are finished. Let them talk themselves out and know without question that they have been heard. This works in all types of situations.

When I was in television advertising sales, I walked into a business on a cold call in an attempt to meet the owner and help him purchase advertising time on my station. As soon as he discovered my line of work, he began a verbal assault on my profession. He ranted on about why he would never "in a million years" buy TV advertising time.

Despite the natural human urge to react, to snap back at him or defend my position, I just let him talk, all the while thinking to myself, "Well, *this* sale isn't going to happen." After a while, his tone began to soften. He started talking about a friend who had done well through television advertising, and I began thinking, "I don't believe this—he's going to buy after all." And he did. Without my saying one word!

Does it always work out like that? No, but letting people talk themselves out is a good beginning, and you never know.

After the person finishes speaking, it's great to let him know you understand his concerns. Remember the *feel, felt, found* we discussed earlier? Use that, and then ask if there are any additional *questions* he might have.

Note that using the word "questions" here, rather than "problems," is much more effective. When they say they don't have any, you're in an excellent position to handle the situation in any way you may deem effective.

You Know a Lot More about This than I Do

One extremely effective phrase is, "You know a lot more about this than I do—how would *you* approach...?" and then fill in the rest with your particular challenge.

You've paid that person's ego a very high compliment and put him in control. Usually, that person will be only too glad to live up to the high level of expectation you've just set for him.

Begin a Criticism with Genuine and Sincere Praise

Another method Dale Carnegie addressed in *How to Win Friends and Influence People* is a very effective way of dispensing criticism without eliciting resentment: begin your criticism with praise.

Note that the praise *must* be genuine and sincere, or it will likely fall upon deaf ears. But if a person first hears something nice and positive about herself, she will be less defensive and feel better about the words of correction that will follow.

Then, after saying what must be said, finish with another kind word or positive thought.

Here's an example: "Don, one thing I've always admired about you is the hard work and pride that you usually put into your projects. That's why I was a bit surprised that the project you just completed was far below your usual standards. It's happened to all of us at one time or another, and I know you well enough to know that's not going to happen again."

What you've done is complimented Don and then criticized not him but his performance. You let him know it's happened to you, too, so he's not alone and doesn't feel singled out. You then complimented him again, while giving an underlying hint that better things are definitely expected.

Regardless of the situation or circumstances in which you use apply this, it will motivate the other person to perform correctly in the future.

Seven Words that Will Come Back to Haunt You

There are seven words that will eventually come back to haunt you sooner or later, especially if said after not treating a person with the proper respect and sense of human dignity. Here are those seven words:

I'll never need him for anything anyway.

Help Them to Be Happy to Do What They Don't Want to Do

True persuasion is being so skillful as to help a person totally change their attitude about a certain position, task, or situation. Here's a great example:

Years ago, when I first began appearing on a number of the major sales and motivational rally programs throughout the country, I would be the opening speaker for either a major sports figure or a more well-known professional speaker than myself. He or she would be the person whose big name would draw the crowd, and I would give the audience the how-to information on business networking, my main topic.

One person was promoting a series of programs to take place monthly in the same city. Included in the twelve-month advertising materials were some of the most famous names in the speaking profession...and there was *me*. Actually, I was totally excited to even to be included in the promotional materials—talk about a thrill for a young speaker! Thirteen speakers were listed in all. Every speaker would have the stage to himself for the entire evening except two: the speaker I would open for, and of course, myself. Ours would be the very first program in the twelve-month series.

When that speaker—an excellent speaker, by the way—saw the schedule, he immediately called the promoter (ego in the lead here) to ask why he was the only major speaker who had to have an opener. Didn't the promoter think he was good enough to carry the program by himself?

The promoter, thinking quickly, told him it was because he was so well-known and I wasn't, and that I needed a big name to establish my credibility—especially for this all-important first program of the series. Our excellent (and formerly ego-wounded) speaker, gladly accepted that with a smile and was fine to do his program, which of all things was on "How to Improve Your Self-Esteem." (Just kidding about the title. That would have been funny, though.)

Declining a Worthless Offer Graciously

When involved in a negotiation and you're offered something you feel holds no value for you, offer lavish appreciation anyway for their thinking of you.

*I'm honored to even be thought of in that way; however,
it wouldn't be feasible in this case.*

Those offering will understand they are way off base as
far as any chance of making a deal with you, but you haven't
offended them with your response.

So many people offend the other person when turning down
an offer—and it just closes doors and makes for a loss for everyone. If you employ tact, you let others save face, and if it's
at all possible, they'll come back with a more realistic offer.

Keeping the Door Open without Being at All Committal

Receiving a call from the decision-maker of a rather
large company to whom I'd been referred, it was quickly obvious that my speaking fee was something with which we
would not be able to come to terms. His last comment to
me was to feel free to call him if I decided I could do their
program for the fee he offered.

Immediately after the conversation, I wrote a thank-
you letter. In this brief, handwritten note, I thanked him
for his call and mentioned nothing whatsoever about the
fee, instead genuinely wishing him a successful convention.
Basically, I said no without in any way closing the door to
further discussion.

This nice but noncommittal note left open the possibility of his calling me back, if he decided he could pay me the
fee I offered. In other words, he could feel comfortable calling me, knowing he wouldn't have to eat humble pie.

Did he call? No, he didn't. However, others in similar situations absolutely have. And regardless of whether he or not he does, the principle worked.

It's much better than closing the door or giving in and selling yourself short.

Notice Something of Their Interest

If at all possible, notice something which is of interest to or a source of pride for the other person. A picture of their child on their desk. Trophies on the wall. Something ...*anything*. But your interest must be genuine, or they'll pick up on your insincerity for sure.

One gentleman was in a position to give me a key referral that would have benefited me greatly in my business. He invited me to his home to discuss the matter with him, letting me know, however, that he was not promising me anything.

He was a retired businessman, and as we walked through his garage, the first thing I noticed was a huge display of hand-carved wooden birds. They were fascinating, beautiful, and exquisitely made.

"Did you carve those yourself?" I asked. Guess what we talked about for the next two hours?

Did I get the referral? I sure did.

It turned out that in his retirement, he made these carvings pretty much day and night. The wooden birds were absolutely incredible. They were also now his primary measurement of self-worth and a powerful source of satisfaction after a long and distinguished career in business.

Notice what is important or of interest to the other person, and you'll be well on your way to mastering the art of persuasion—effortlessly!

Yet Another Reason to Smile

Smile as you are saying something constructive to someone, particularly when you are telling them something that, if you *weren't* smiling, could be interpreted as an insult. If you can smile while doing this, it's one of the best ways to build a person while at the same time being constructive.

Picture me smiling as I tell Ken he's not speaking with enough respect to his associate:

See, Ken, when we do that, we usually get the exact opposite response than we want from the other person.

This comes across a lot differently than if I had given him a disgusted look and said the same thing. Practice this. It really works!

My Dad is absolutely the *best* in the world at this. Fortunately, I've been able to acquire this skill after much practice.

We're not talking here about giving mixed signals (smiling while angry or something similar), but about using your smile simply to soften a criticism. You know it's working when the person begins to unconsciously mirror your smile—he or she smiles back at you while being taught.

What a win that is!

Know Your Objective and Plan Your Approach

Milo Frank, in his book *How to Make Your Point in 30 Seconds or Less*, talks about knowing your objective and then planning your approach. When your objective, for example, is to get back the money you spent on a defective product, or to get an exchange on an item you purchased, you need to have an effective, planned approach.

You begin with, "I know good companies like yours stand behind their merchandise."

What has Mr. Frank suggested here? Basically, that you are giving them something of high value, such as their excellent reputation, to live up to.

I really like his quote:

> Know what you want, know who can give it
> to you, and know how to get it.

This applies to achieving your goals in practically anything you undertake.

Doing Business for This Price Is an Insurance Policy

During a negotiation, another way of warning someone without actually threatening him (remember the implied threat) is what I call the "insurance policy technique."

Once, while negotiating the price of a car, I told the car salesperson the following (with tact, of course):

"Mr. Kennedy, if we can't agree on this particular price, I can't justify making the purchase right now without investigating further.

"I'm not saying that I won't eventually come back here. I enjoy working with you—but I'd have to visit several other dealerships to see if I could get the price I feel I need...."

Okay, here it comes:

"In a sense," I continued, "your coming down XX amount of dollars right now is sort of like"—this is said with a sincere smile—"you buying an insurance policy that I *won't* buy the car from someone else. Of course, I'll understand if you just can't do that."

As I began, I said what I needed to say with a look of kindness, not a scowl. And I told him I couldn't "justify" making the purchase now—not that I *won't* make the purchase. I wanted to help him save face and have him want to help me get what I wanted.

What was the result?

I got my price. And it was a win/win. The dealer and salesperson still made a healthy profit, and that sale resulted in several referrals from me to that salesperson. The transaction was handled in a professional way, and that scenario positively set up my next visit. He knows that if I don't get the price I feel I need, I won't be able to *justify* making the purchase now.

The Compliment Game

In *How to Have Confidence and Power in Dealing with People*, Les Giblin advises us to form the habit of paying at least three sincere compliments each day. Good idea.

Mr. Giblin talks about syndicated columnist Dr. George Crane suggesting people join what he calls The Compliment Club. To be a member, all a person has to do is deliberately go out and search for good things in other people that they can compliment.

As training for mastering the art of persuasion, you can make a game out of it and call it The Compliment Game.

How many days in a row can you go, giving out at least—*at least*—five compliments a day? That's one or more compliments, to five different people, each and every day.

Your only competition is yourself, and if you win the game, imagine how much more effective your powers of positive persuasion will become.

Be the Host, Not the Guest

In my book *Endless Referrals*, I discuss the strategy of positioning yourself as one of the "big men/women on campus," also known as *playing the host, not the guest*.

When you're in a situation where you can introduce people to each other, by all means do so. A person may attend an event and be too bashful to go right up and introduce themselves to people they don't know. Go out of your way to do this for them. Tell each person what the other does for a living and highlight a couple of their interests.

Once, after receiving a referral from someone I had met only once, I asked why he thought of me. He replied that he had attended a meeting of an association to which I belong. It was his first time there, and while everyone else practically ignored him, I made him feel like part of the crowd, introducing him around and making sure he was always involved in the conversation.

Little things like that get noticed. That's not why you do them. But they do get noticed, and often with terrific results.

The One Key Question

In *Endless Referrals*, I also discuss what I call the One Key Question that will set you apart from all the rest. It will also help you persuade, in the long-term and sometimes right away, too, depending on the circumstances.

After finding out what a person does for a living, I'll usually ask a couple of what I call *Feel-Good Questions*. These are questions that are very nonsalesy; they are not intrusive or invasive, and simply make the person feel good about being asked. They might include asking how they got their start in the business they are in and what they enjoy most about it.

I'll then ask the following, what I call the "One Key Question" that will set you appart from the rest:

Joe, how can I know if someone I'm talking to would be a good prospect for you?

Think about what your response would be if someone asked you that question. What would you think? How would you feel about that person?

That's a question that will never offend anyone, and will always be much appreciated. Most people have never been asked that question, and knowing you are a possible referral source—or that you even cared enough to ask—will certainly make them want to go out of their way to please you. Of course, if you can ever do it, make sure to actually refer business their way. What a great way to provide them with value!

You can also adapt the essential premise of that question to any particular situation in which you are involved. For instance, "Hey, Mary, how can I know if someone I'm talking to would be a good contact for you in helping your son find a summer job?"

The chances are excellent that Mary will hold you in high regard and most likely be happy to assist you in your endeavors.

Addressing the Superior

There are times you must go over a person's head (nicely, of course) and summon the manager.

You can do this tactfully by saying, "I understand that you want to help and that it's a difficult situation. I certainly don't want to get you in hot water or put you on the spot in any way. I'd actually feel more comfortable discussing this with your manager." Make sure to ask the manager's name—including her last name—before she is summoned.

When the manager arrives, she may assume you're like most people—ready to take her head off. Don't be surprised if she starts out a bit defensively. Your attitude with the person who had to get her will probably help, but assume he just went back and like most people said, "We have a customer with a problem."

Realize you may be dealing with a person who is expecting an argument. Have your sincere, warm smile ready to disarm. Say, "Hi, Ms. Jackson." (Please, use last names whenever you can. It shows respect.) Shake her hand with a firm but nonaggressive grip. Smile and look in her eyes as you say her name.

"I'm Bob Burg, thank you for seeing me, I know you're very busy."

What have you done? You've totally disarmed that person and put her in a win/win frame of mind. Now you can make your case on a level playing field—or even better, one slanted significantly in your favor.

Giblin's Truth Serum

In Les Giblin's book *How to Have Confidence and Power in Dealing with People,* he shows that the best way to move someone to act in a particular way is to let them live up to your opinion of them. He provides several wonderful examples of people who were trusted and lived up to the trust placed in them.

One story tells of a police officer who was consistently able to get thugs to give him information. How? By saying, "People tell me you have quite a reputation as a tough guy, and that you've been in lots of trouble, but there's one thing you won't do. You won't lie. They say, if you tell me anything at all, it will be the truth—and that's the reason I'm here." Wow, talk about giving a person something to live up to!

Les quotes famed British statesman Sir Winston Churchill as saying, "I have found that the best way to get another to acquire a virtue is to impute it to him."

As I've suggested, gear these methods to your own unique circumstances. Not just to see if they work—they do!—but to practice getting really good at making them work for you in a variety of situations.

The first time I read about this, I couldn't wait to try it out.

My first opportunity was with a person who trying to get some information for me. I had used her services before and she always did a good job. Not great, but good. This time, though, she was having some trouble, and I said to the person next to me (within this person's earshot), "I don't know if this information can be found or not, but I'll tell you this—if anyone can find it, she can."

You can bet your boots she found it, and now she goes out of her way for me whenever I need to stop by.

The "Negative Yes"

I learned the following from the great speaker and sales trainer Tom Hopkins, author of the outstanding book, *How to Master the Art of Selling*. Tom suggests, when trying to set an appointment for something that a person usually resists, phrasing your question in the form of a negative so that a "no" answer serves the same purpose as a "yes" response. This works best when the person is used to saying, and almost automatically answers "no."

Confusing? Here's how it works:

A Realtor® wanting to visit a seller who is planning to sell her home without professional assistance might ask over the telephone, "Ms. Davis, would you be offended if I popped by to see your home?" When she says, "No," she's really saying "Yes, come on over."

The brilliance of this lies in how the question was framed in the first place. Had he said the usual, "May I stop by to see your home?" then the "no" answer would have truly meant no. But instead, the question he asked allowed the seller to say "no" (which she was probably all primed and ready to say, no matter what the question was!) and still have it mean *yes!*

The "negative yes" technique won't necessarily work every time, but it will swing the odds more in your favor.

When attempting to persuade by getting a person to consider something you need, simply ask, "Would you be offended if…?" and finish your request. There's a very good chance you'll get a "no"—which of course means a winning "yes"!

Plant the Affirmative

Let's say you're going to ask someone out on a dinner date. Which of these three ways do you think would elicit the most positive response:

"You wouldn't want to go out to dinner with me, would you?"

"Would you like to go out to dinner with me?"

"If we were to go to dinner, where would you most like to go?"

Number three is the only question that is set up so that the "yes" response is already planted within the answer. If the person you are asking responds by saying, "Oh, I'd like to go to the Lobster House," then what they have actually said is, "Yes, I'd like to go out with you to the Lobster House."

Obviously, that was intended to be a fun (albeit facetious) example. And I'll readily admit I have never personally asked a woman out that way, but that's only because I'm not that brave! Still, you know, it might be fun to see what happens…

Getting the Cab Driver on Your Side

If you are leaving your hotel in the morning and catching a cab to the airport, here's a way to get the driver on your side, have a smooth, pleasant ride, and ensure that you're treated right: as you leave the hotel, offer the cab driver a cup of coffee.

Hotels often provide free coffee in the morning, and it's okay to take one for the driver. And even if you do have to pay for it, it's still a good investment. You're most likely the only passenger who has ever shown the driver such respect, and he'll really appreciate it.

When you're zipping around in that rush-hour traffic, it isn't a bad idea to have him on your side.

And, as you know, just for its own sake, it's simply a really nice thing to do for another human being.

Compliment the Uncomplimented

Go out of your way to compliment those people who serve others but are not usually acknowledged, let alone treated with respect. From the waitperson to the skycaps (aside from tipping them), do you refer to them as "Sir" or "Ma'am"? Not only is it the right way to behave toward other people, but, yes, it makes a definite difference in how far out of their way they'll go for you.

A great illustration of this showcases the people skills of the great former quarterback and highly successful entrepreneur Fran Tarkenton.

As a quarterback, and a small one at only five foot ten, Fran was always the target of huge, tough, often merciless defensive linemen. Linemen can be mean to a quarterback. They're supposed to be. It's their job. What's more, they know they don't earn the kind of money most quarterbacks do, and they certainly don't enjoy the same praises and glory. Those three-hundred-pound guys can be downright rough on the Fran Tarkentons of the world.

But Fran is a master at dealing with people—a maestro of the art of persuasion. According to his former teammate, Ahmad Rashad, after a play, he'd acknowledge his attacker by saying something like, "Great day for football, isn't it?" or "Man, that was quite a hit."

These guys weren't exactly used to quarterbacks actually talking to them (at least not in anything other than four-letter words), and they certainly weren't used to being treated as human beings. Before long, they were no longer quite as aggressive, mean, and nasty with Fran. They'd still hit him, of course, but they wouldn't rough him up as they did other quarterbacks.

He took the anger out of them and probably added years to his Hall of Fame career.

That sure is one situation when the ability to persuade *really* comes in handy—when your life depends upon it!

Shaking Hands

The way you shake hands is important. Typically, a firm but not crunching or aggressive handshake is best. Look the person in the eye and smile a genuine, happy-to-meet-you smile.

Dad taught us kids how to shake hands and introduce ourselves when we were still practically babies, and it's a skill I've often been complimented on throughout my life.

Another great way of shaking hands I've learned from observing successful people is to use a double hand clasp, with your two hands sandwiching theirs, and give a slight bow of your head. That tells a person they must be very special.

It's another win, *hands down*.

Attitude

When you're about to solicit someone's help, assume that person will indeed be helpful and not obstructive.

Here's the remarkable thing about how this works: whichever attitude you expect him to take will show up in your attitude toward him—and he will usually respond in kind, precisely according to your attitude.

It's yet another example of getting what you expect.

Reintroduce Yourself

Making other people feel comfortable with you is one sure step to both short- and long-term success with people. One great way to do this is to reintroduce yourself to people you've previously met—even if you think they ought to know your name already.

We all forget names sometimes, and one of the most uncomfortable feelings in the world is to have someone approach you whose name you should know—but don't. It's even worse if you're with one or two people to whom you're expected to introduce this person. Ouch.

Has anyone ever approached you whose name you couldn't remember? Have you ever approached someone who should know your name, but you are sure (or at least you suspect) that she doesn't?

Here's the most effective way I know of to handle this situation, and you'll score big points with that person when you use it: simply reintroduce yourself.

It's as easy as that.

"Hi, Nancy, Bob Burg." Or even, "Hi, Nancy, Bob Burg, we met at the Save-a-Pet fundraiser two weeks ago."

What I've done is I've given Nancy an out. I've allowed her—and her ego—to save face. Now she doesn't have to be uncomfortable with me or herself. And she'll usually respond by saying, "Sure, Bob, I remember you."

Now, I know she didn't remember my name. And she knows she didn't remember my name. She might even know that I know she didn't remember my name. It doesn't matter. Making that reintroduction most definitely reestablished her know you, like you, trust you feelings—and doing that will go a long way toward helping you master the art of persuasion.

F-O-R-M

A great idea, first brought to my attention years ago by super-entrepreneur Dexter Yager, is the F-O-R-M method of asking questions. This acronym helps focus your attention on what might be important to the other person:

"F" stands for (their) Family.

"O" stands for (their) Occupation.

"R" stands for (their) favorite types of Recreation.

"M" stands for (their) Message, that is, what they deem important.

Here is an additional tip: if you want to learn more but they've stopped talking, just say, "Really, tell me more…" When was the last time you had a conversation with someone who was so genuinely curious about you he or she wanted to know *more*?

When you focus on the other person during a conversation and ask about what is important to *them*, you are always in good FORM.

Understanding

You've seen throughout this book how people like to feel that they are heard and understood. Regardless of the situation, people will make more of an effort on your behalf when they feel you understand their personal challenges.

Make it a point not only to understand that person, but to do so in such a way that the person *knows* you understand. That can make all the difference in the world in your efforts to persuade for everyone's benefit.

Solicit Their Opinion

When trying to persuade people the see your point of view and take the action you want them to take, you'll find that the more you ask them for their opinion and counsel, the more they'll be on your side.

One of the best examples of this I ever saw was years ago, back when I was in college, at a speech given by Senator Ted Kennedy.

Facing a crowd that was somewhat challenging in nature, the senator took an informal poll regarding an issue that was very controversial at the time. He actually asked the audience members who felt a certain way about the subject to raise their hands. He made the audience feel he was asking for and actually *cared* about our opinion. From that point on, the audience was much more receptive.

Have you ever heard the saying, first said by the late, great Cavett Robert, "People don't care how much you know, until they know how much you care"? The senator did just that with the entire audience.

I've used this approach of soliciting advice from prospects (whether or not I necessarily felt I actually needed the advice in question) and others throughout the years, and it has most definitely served as a very effective persuasion tool. And here's a way to enhance its power even further: after securing the desired results, make that person feel that the ideas were *theirs* and that they contributed greatly to your success.

By the way, even though I mentioned that I don't necessarily feel I need the asked-for advice, that doesn't mean I might not learn something valuable in the process. In fact, I almost certainly will. The more you ask, in fact, the more you actually *will* learn—and the chances are good that they genuinely *will* end up making a contribution to your success.

Les Giblin suggests asking someone specifically for *advice*, rather than asking for a *favor*. That's an excellent idea. For example, let's say you want to get your son a summer job at the Jones company, and a neighbor of yours, who you know by name but don't know *that* well, is in upper management there and could probably help.

You probably feel (correctly) that it would be too presumptuous of you to simply walk up and ask your neighbor to get your boy a job. So instead, you ask him for advice. "Don, if you don't mind my asking, if you were me and were going to attempt to get your son set up with a summer job at the Jones company, what do you feel would be the most effective way to go about it?"

Don, who is now being asked for counsel (and *not* for a favor), might just tell you to send your son down to his office on Monday, and he'll see what he can do. Or maybe he'll give you the Jones company personnel manager's name and number, and tell you to use him as a referral. At the least, he'll almost certainly lead you in the right direction.

Just remember to phrase your request something similar to: "Phyllis, if you were me and were attempting to [do whatever it is you're wanting to do], how would you go about it?" Or, "Joe, I'd like to get your opinion on something. What would you do if [he were in your situation]?"

It's another easy yet powerful way to set up a big win.

10

Beyond Business

Don't Embarrass Someone by "Catching" Them

Does it ever do any good to embarrass someone, either publicly or privately? No, I don't believe it does any good anytime, but especially not if you are ever planning to win this person over and have them on your side. Embarrassing a person by "catching" them at something is a sure way to shoot yourself in the foot—or worse.

I was in a conversation once with a group of several people at a social gathering and when asked a question, I answered by repeating a very funny line I had heard on a recent television show. Everyone laughed, and I admit, I accepted the laughter *without* explaining that I had actually borrowed that joke, and it wasn't something I came up with on the spur of the moment through my own brilliance.

One of the people in the group had seen the same program—and they called me on it right then and there, in front of everyone. It was embarrassing, and although I was wrong not to have given credit to the show myself, it certainly did not endear that person to me.

What did that person gain by embarrassing me? Nothing but perhaps a brief, fleeting moment of satisfaction. Remember the ego?

On the other hand, when I was in college, we had a guest speaker named Bill Lee. A former star major league pitcher for the Boston Red Sox, Bill was known as "Spaceman" for his unusual personality. Before the speech, about thirty of us had a private welcoming party for Bill.

At the party, I said something that was meant to be funny, but it just didn't go over. The room fell silent. It was more than a silence: it was one of those truly *embarrassing* silences.

And then, without missing a beat, Bill stepped right in and segued from my dumb joke into a story, totally taking the heat off me and dissolving that embarrassing feeling right away.

From that day on, I have been a *big* Bill Lee fan.

What Not to Do in Order to Effectively Persuade

At some of my speaking engagements, my clients will assign a host to make sure that I get to where I need to be and that I am taken care of during my stay. One client in particular provides this courtesy quite often, for which I'm very grateful, and the hosts are always nice people who go out of their way to make sure all is okay, from accommodations to transportation.

After one presentation that ran well into the evening, my host and I went to the hotel restaurant to see if we could get a couple of sandwiches. The restaurant had just closed. Typically, I'm too keyed up to eat before a program, but afterward I'm often very hungry. I sure could have used a sandwich right about then.

By the time we got to the place, the only person in the front dining room was the manager. Everyone else was either gone or in the kitchen cleaning up. The manager was across the room from us, and my host—a really nice guy— got the manager's attention by yelling, "Yo!"

Ouch. I was immediately embarrassed, and it was obvious that the manager wasn't any more pleased than I. As he turned around, I could see a very annoyed look on his face which seemed to say, "I can't believe I have to put up with people like this." He didn't actually say that, but the expression on his face sure did.

He responded by sarcastically saying, "Yo! How can I help you?"

Funny, when my host asked if we could get a couple of sandwiches, the answer was that they were already closed. Surprise, surprise!

I was eventually able to get the sandwiches made, but I really had my work cut out for me. First I had undo the damage done by my well-intentioned host, and then go about winning over the manager. Finally he told me that if the ingredients had not yet been put away, he would see to it that we got them.

We did ultimately get to eat our sandwiches. But how unnecessary the challenge was, when a simple, respectful greeting in the first place would have done the trick and made for an easy win.

Even Kids Can Win Without Intimidation

My sister Robyn related this story to me about my niece, Samantha, who was then eight years old. I was very proud of the way she handled the situation.

Samantha had one of her little friends over to the house to play. They were getting along fine, when the friend began to get cranky, as eight-year-olds will. They had agreed to go outside to play, when all of a sudden the little friend yelled, "I'm not going outside to play with you!"

Sami kept her head—responding, not reacting—and very nicely said, "Okay, well I'm going outside anyway," and she began to walk away. She took a couple more steps, and just as she reached the door, she stopped, turned around, and said, "but it won't be as much fun without you."

According to Robyn, the little friend's eyes just lit up, and she decided to join Samantha outside after all. Robyn said she thought I'd be proud of Sami for that. She was right. Actually, I'm *always* proud of Samantha and my nephew Mark—but I was especially proud of the way she so gracefully demonstrated the art of persuasion.

The Positive Challenge

Give a person a challenge framed in a positive manner, and they will often go out of their way for you in order to meet that challenge.

My good friend Monte Johnson and his wife Cindy needed quick invitations to a wedding shower. They were having no success at all with the local printers. Cindy was pleading, "We really need to get these today. We're in an emergency situation." The response she got? "Sorry, there is no way we could possibly do that." (How original, right?)

If you look at this situation closely, you can see that when Cindy said, "We really need to get these today," she was in fact being *I-oriented*. Now, you might think that should be okay in this case; after all, she's the paying customer. But as we discover anew every day, people don't do things *logically*, they do things *emotionally*.

She also asked the question in such a way that it didn't set a frame for the printer to provide a solution. But watch how her husband does it.

Monte, who intuitively employs a lot of the methods we've been discussing in this book, told me he got on the phone with the next printer and simply asked, "What's the fastest you've ever gotten invitations out?" The response was, "Oh, we can probably get them out today."

Isn't that amazing? It is—but it doesn't surprise those of us who do this every day. This is simply the way to elicit people working with you rather than against you.

What was the difference in focus in the way that Monte made his request? He was *you-oriented*. "What's the fastest *you've* ever gotten invitations out?" Just as importantly, the 'very way he asked the question provided a frame for the answer to be a positive response.

Monte, who is in video production and records large conventions, often finds himself in a new town and needing to get an item in a hurry, such as a banner. He'll call a company that supplies banners and ask, "If there's any way you could help me out—this just got dropped on my lap and your help would really be appreciated. In fact, if there's any extra charge, that's fine."

Monte tells me (and I believe it, because I do this myself all the time) that his success rate is almost 100 percent—and he hardly ever has to pay anything extra.

Giving Before Receiving

In persuading over the long haul, you'll find that the more you're willing to give to others—without attachment to the results—the more you'll receive in return. A great example of this is my friend and client, Ron Hale of Tennessee. Ron is an extremely successful businessman who practiced the art of giving without attachment to instant rewards while still in the armed forces.

As an Air Force recruiter, it was Ron's job to sell young people on why they should join the service and serve their country while creating a good life foundation for themselves. Before he could sell them on anything, though, he first had to get in front of them, and that could be a difficult task. To make matters even more challenging, he was located in a town that was filled with Navy people.

Ron knew that one key to his success was developing centers of influence who could serve as good sources of referrals—people who might actually send good candidates to him. But how could he develop relationships with these influencers without becoming a bother to them, causing negative feelings?

Here Ron perfectly used his natural inclination to give freely, simply for the sake of adding value to others. Still, the result would be countless referrals and opportunities for free publicity from some of the most important centers of influence in town.

During his weekly itinerary, Ron would visit such places as schools, radio stations, television stations, and the local newspaper. When stopping by, he would never mention anything about recruiting or referrals. He would simply strike up a friendly chat and then find a way he could help *them*.

For instance, he would bring the person at the radio station the newest Air Force band records for them to play whenever they liked. To the administrators and teachers at the schools, he'd bring in Air Force book covers that would help prolong the life of the books.

There was a young minister with a very small television station that was often left with lots of dead air time. What would Ron bring him? Air Force films with entertaining footage that could fill up lots of time. Every so often, the young, up-and-coming minister would run Air Force ads right on the air.

All the while, Ron never once asked for a referral. But to whom do you think those folks sent all the young people they felt should check out the armed services? Ron was building a huge referral business simply by cultivating giving relationships with these major local influencers.

One holiday season, the editor of the local newspaper in this primarily Navy town decided to ask an armed forces representative for a story regarding military personnel at Christmas. Instead of asking someone from the Navy, he asked Ron. Soon after that, Ron and his family were the focus of a feature story in that very same newspaper. According to Ron, that one story was worth its weight in gold in free advertising.

Remember the young television minister whom Ron helped out by constantly bringing in films about the Air Force to help the dead air time? As he grew bigger and better known, he remembered Ron and gave him more and more free publicity. You'd probably agree that he actually got fairly big. His name is Pat Robertson.

I've had the pleasure of getting to know Ron and his lovely wife Toby. They both embody the spirit of giving, and by consistently giving without an attachment to immediate results, they have built an enormous network marketing organization that literally spans the globe.

Give, give, and give some more, and ultimately you will find yourself *receiving* more than you ever thought possible.

Saying "No" to Charity Telephone Solicitations with Class and Kindness

It happens to us all. In the middle of dinner or while relaxing with our family, the telephone rings, and on the other end is a nice person reading from a script asking us to make a financial donation to the very worthwhile charitable cause he or she is representing.

This, in and of itself, is fine (providing that it's a legitimate charity, of course!). If you want to make a donation to that particular cause, fantastic. I know that many of us truly enjoy donating to causes we believe in.

However, let's face it, it's difficult to donate a significant amount of money to every charitable organization in the world. And I don't know about you, but it seems as though I'm called by just about every one of them.

How do you say "no" nicely, without being rude or slamming down the phone, discouraging another human being from doing their job. Here's how I do it, and it's proven very effective.

I let them finish their short presentation and then respond by saying, "I appreciate your call. I do, however, have several charities to which I donate, and although I'm contacted by many very worthwhile causes, such as yours, I have made the decision to stick with the ones I've chosen." Then I add, "But I do appreciate your call and wish you the best of success in your work. Thank you very much for your time."

Respond this way, and nine times out of ten they'll thank you for *your* time and then hang right up. Or, if they do try one more time, such as, "Well, sir, just a very small donation would really help..." I let them complete their sentence and then say, "I appreciate your offer, but again, that is the decision I've made. Best of success, though. Have a great night."

That will do it. There's no reason to say you don't want to, can't afford it, or anything else. That's not really any of anyone else's beeswax. The answer I just gave is polite, encouraging, and more than satisfactory—because when you both can't win, making sure no one loses is a great second best.

Many times I've had telephone solicitors actually thank me for my politeness and encouragement instead of the rudeness they're often shown by people. What a great feeling to know you're making a positive difference in someone's life.

Setting an Example People Will Follow

My good friend, Vic Landtroop, related a couple of stories to me about how doing what is right—instead of what is usual—can be a positive influence that others will duplicate. Both examples happened at a college football game between two great rivals, the University of Florida and the University of Tennessee.

Vic and his business associate Bubba Pratt, two of Bubba's young children, and another friend all drove up from Florida to Tennessee in Bubba's custom-built luxury coach to see the game. It would be a record-breaking crowd and the parking lot was filled to capacity with fans from both schools having a huge tailgating party before the early afternoon game.

As Vic says, often in that kind of situation there's a lot of disrespect back and forth between the fans of the rival teams. In fact, three Tennessee Volunteer supporters who were drinking beer over their hibachi and already feeling their oats looked over and made a somewhat sarcastic remark about the Florida Gators.

Vic and Bubba decided to take the high road. The two were complimentary toward the other team. "We have a lot of respect for the guys on your team," they told the Tennessee fans. "They're super folks in our eyes." They approached the situation the right way—not out of weakness, but out of strength. (Incidentally, Bubba is a former Gator linebacker and a martial artist, and Vic is a former professional wrestler.)

Remember the saying from Simeon ben Zoma, "A mighty person is one who can control his emotions and make of an enemy a friend." That's just what Vic and Bubba did. In fact, they invited the three guys to tour Bubba's custom coach and even offered them some of the food they'd laid out. They treated their guests with class.

Vic says, "It was great—despite the 'cans of courage' they had been drinking, they kept telling us what super guys we were."

After the game (which Florida won), the three Volunteer fans sought Vic and Bubba out and complimented them on the Gator win with comments such as, "Hey, the best team won. We hope you go all the way."

What a great job of setting a positive example that others can follow, by treating people with respect instead of falling into the customary reactive trap of insult and rivalry. I believe Vic and Bubba's attitude really set the stage for influencing the behavior of those other fans.

Vic related another story to me that shows the same kind of positive impact you can have when you choose to lead in a positive direction.

As the fans were walking to the stadium, they had to come down a very steep slope in the pathway. Bubba, who is a real gentleman, first noticed that the men were not helping the women, some of whom were having trouble with their footing on the steep grade. According to Vic, "It was like every man—and woman—for themselves. As soon as Bubba started helping people, practically everyone else, men and women alike, began lending a helping hand."

Isn't it great to know we can all make a real difference by reaching out just a little? People will follow others who set a positive example.

Vic says we all need to read *How to Win Friends and Influence People* and other books on personal growth. "I never knew about these tools when I was growing up," he told me. "I'm glad to be raising my kids and know that I'm able to expose them to these resources while they're still young."

Personal growth for generations to come. What a great concept!

The Importance of Humor in Winning without Intimidation

Maybe it goes without saying but humor—kind humor, not sarcastic humor—can often go a long way toward getting what you want through effective persuasion.

I'm very comfortable with self-deprecating humor. In a tense situation, I often make myself the object of humor. "Umh, I can't believe I lost this ticket. I literally would lose my head if it weren't attached to my neck." That puts the other person just a little bit closer to my side of the challenge.

If you're not comfortable laughing at yourself (I am because there's a lot to laugh about), then make fun of the situation itself—though of course only if that's appropriate and will help your cause.

If you're not a naturally funny or humorous person, don't feel you need to force humor, because if you do, it will typically have the opposite effect. However, if you can downplay the seriousness or make light of the situation, it will definitely help you in your quest toward persuading the other person to your side of the issue.

Treat Your Suppliers the Same Way You Treat Your Customers and Clients

To ensure a wonderful relationship with your suppliers, one in which you get special, preferential treatment, and especially in those situations where it is badly needed, be sure to build a strong foundation.

How? By treating them with all the respect most people normally reserve only for their paying customers. Ask yourself the following questions:

Do you pay your suppliers on time?

Do you talk *with* them rather than *at* them?

Do you discuss challenges instead of demanding and yelling?

Do you refer others to them, if and when appropriate?

If you answered "yes" to those questions, you are on your way to earning that special place in their hearts that will elicit consistent efforts on your behalf—especially in those minor emergencies where the average person may not get that same satisfaction.

That's the essence of positive persuasion.

Keeping Cool Behind the Wheel

You might not immediately recognize the name of my good friend Ralph Lagergren, but you may have read about him in *People* magazine, or in the book based on the success story of Ralph and his cousin, Mark Underwood.

Mark invented, and Ralph sold and marketed, a more efficient grain reaper that could outperform the standard machines sold by the larger, more established farm implement companies. The book about their venture, *Dream Reaper*, written by Craig Canine, is great reading. It's truly an American success story involving our wonderful system of free enterprise and the good that can result when you combine a big dream with ingenuity and hard work.

Ralph is one of those guys you immediately like, and a man who also believes in the benefits of winning without intimidation.

One day, as Ralph was driving along with his two kids, he stopped at a red light. Behind him was a man driving a Volkswagen, and through his rearview mirror Ralph could tell the guy was mad at him. Although Ralph didn't know what he had clone to elicit such angry feelings—possibly he stopped too short or too abruptly—he could see the man gesturing and mouthing words that didn't look like roses, if you know what I mean.

Ralph is a big ol' Kansas cowboy and not the type you want to pick a fight with. But he also had two young children in the car with him, and besides, Ralph would rather handle situations like this in the correct way.

When the light turned green, Ralph began driving— and he could see right away the Volkswagen pulling up to him. Ralph warned the kids that this man might make an unfriendly gesture and that the three of them would respond with a friendly smile and a wave. That's exactly what happened and, according to Ralph, the face of the man in the Volkswagen turned from angry to somewhat confused.

Wouldn't you know that at the next traffic signal the light turned red, and the two cars pulled up right next to each other. When the man looked over, a bit embarrassed, Ralph smiled that big ol' cowboy smile at him again. The man, startled again, asked if they knew each other. Ralph replied, "No, we don't know each other, but life is just too short to let things like traffic misunderstandings get in the way of enjoying myself."

Two months later, Ralph was stopped at another red light, driving a different car. All of a sudden, that same Volkswagen pulled up beside him and the man in the car, remembering his face, waved and smiled at his new friend.

What an excellent example Ralph set for his children on how, with a little bit of thought and effort, one person can make the world a better place for others as well as one-self. Ralph was the mightier man for it, wasn't he? Because he controlled his emotions and made of an enemy a friend. That's the art of persuasion at its finest.

The Art of Persuasion to Get Backstage

Here's another Ralph Lagergren story:

Ralph's wife, Dawn, is a big fan of country singer and musician George Strait. When the former Entertainer of the Year was making an appearance in Ralph's town, Ralph thought of a great surprise he could give his wife: an opportunity to meet Mr. Strait backstage before his concert. Aside from the fact that lots of people would like to get backstage at concerts, Ralph knew that another major challenge is that this singing superstar has a policy of seeing only two guests backstage per performance.

Ralph, a master at the sort of persuasion we are discussing in this book, sent a letter to the sponsoring radio station expressing that through thick and thin, good times and especially the tough times, Dawn had stood by him. It would be a very special gift to her if she could get a chance to meet Mr. Strait. He added, "I'm not worried about meeting him myself, as I know he only sees two people per show, but it would be just great if I could get this for Dawn."

The station manager called Ralph, saying he had received the letter and found it very interesting and certainly moving. Ralph replied—and these words are key—"*I want to thank you for even considering this*. I know it's difficult for you, and there must be thousands of requests like mine. This would just be so special for her."

You can guess the results, can't you? Those words, "I want to thank you for even considering this," work like magic. You are being humble and respectful.

Will that always work? No, not always. Sometimes the situation just won't allow it. However, if there's any chance at all, those words will usually cinch it for you.

At the concert, the public address announcer paged Ms. Dawn Lagergren, asking her to come backstage. What an incredible surprise and gift Ralph was able to give to his best friend and loving wife, because her husband had mastered the art of persuasion.

The Art of Persuasion Dream

I'm the type who really gets into my work. While I was writing this book, the topic consumed my mind, literally day and night. It actually got to the point where I was waking up during the night writing down ideas that would come to me while I was sleeping, and even having story-like dreams about this book.

One of these dreams really made me laugh. It was strange, but it brought up a worthwhile point I want to share with you.

In this dream, there was a helmet with strange powers. Anyone who wore this helmet automatically knew the perfect response to a challenging situation and was in the proper mindset to enact it. When you took the helmet off, that was no longer so, but when you put it back on, you again had the benefits of that super power.

When someone had a challenge with someone else, she would ask for the helmet, put it on—and handle every situation beautifully.

Weird dream? Sure. Weird guy—weird dream. In fact, I remember actually laughing during the dream, right as it was going on, because even then I was thinking how funny it was.

But I believe it made a good point:

If, whenever a challenge with someone comes up, we decide to respond by putting on that helmet before reacting negatively, we will always be in a position of strength and know exactly what to say and how to say it.

The dream may have been a dream, but I think the helmet is real. All it is is a mastery of the art of persuasion.

The Language of Strength

I want to close by reiterating a way to handle yourself and deal with those difficult others I mentioned near the beginning of this book.

This may be the one concept that makes the biggest difference in your ability to persuade others to your way of thinking and attain the results you desire. It is known by several different words: diplomacy, delicacy, sensitivity, savoir-faire, and *tact*.

Tact is the inspired language of strength. Learning what to say and how to say it will get results for you that will seem like magic.

Every situation you find yourself in, and every time you must call someone's attention to a particular way of acting, keep tact in mind. Tact will be the key to how those people receive you and what you have to say, and whether or not that person will ultimately take the action that will benefit all concerned.

When you master the art of tact, you will constantly and consistently find yourself in the position of winning without intimidation.

Just think for a moment: how many of us will it take, responding rather than reacting to the challenges in our work and lives and mastering the art of persuasion—to change the world for the better forever?

About the Author

A former television personality and top-producing sales-person, Bob Burg speaks to corporations and organizations worldwide on topics at the core of *The Art of Persuasion*. Addressing audiences ranging from sixty to sixteen thousand, Bob has shared the platform with some of today's top business leaders, broadcast personalities, coaches, athletes, and political leaders, including a former U.S. president. Bob is also coauthor of the *Wall Street Journal* bestseller *The Go-Giver, Go-Givers Sell More*, and *It's Not About You*. His classic *Endless Referrals* has sold more than two hundred thousand copies and is still used today as a training manual in many corporations.